Making Sense of Sex

Making Sense of Sex

*Responsible Decision Making
for Young Singles*

MICHAEL F. DUFFY

WJK WESTMINSTER
JOHN KNOX PRESS
LOUISVILLE · KENTUCKY

First edition
Published by Westminster John Knox Press
Louisville, Kentucky

11 12 13 14 15 16 17 18 19 20—10 9 8 7 6 5 4 3 2 1

Book design by Sharon Adams
Cover design by Eric Walljasper, Minneapolis, MN

Library of Congress Cataloging-in-Publication Data
Duffy, Michael Frederick.
  Making sense of sex : responsible decision making for young singles / by Michael F. Duffy.—1st ed.
    p. cm.
  Includes bibliographical references (p.   ).
  ISBN 978-0-664-23337-2 (alk. paper)
  1. Christian youth—Religious life.   2. Sex—Religious aspects—Christianity.   3. Decision making—Religious aspects—Christianity.   I. Title.
  BV4531.3.D835   2010
  241'.66—dc22

                                                                                        2010033789

PRINTED IN THE UNITED STATES OF AMERICA

♾ The paper used in this publication meets the minimum requirements of the
American National Standard for Information Sciences—Permanence
of Paper for Printed Library Materials, ANSI Z39.48-1992.

Westminster John Knox Press advocates the responsible use of our natural resources.
The text paper of this book is made from at least 30% post-consumer waste.

Special Sales
Most Westminster John Knox Press books are available at special quantity discounts
when purchased in bulk by corporations, organizations, and special-interest groups.
For more information, please e-mail SpecialSales@wjkbooks.com.

To my wife, Bonnie

Contents

Acknowledgments

A huge number of people have contributed to this book, and I owe thanks to them all.

I thank all of the students who have taken my ThS 326, *Sexual Ethics and the Christian Tradition*, course at Hanover College. The last two or three of these classes have been especially formative for my thinking about the format and content of this book.

I thank the many people who remain totally anonymous in this book but who have given me the invaluable quotations that lie at its heart. Your willingness to share your words is going to help someone out there in the world, even if you never know whom or how. Deep thanks to you. In addition to these anonymous friends, and with my sincerest apologies to anyone I forget to mention here, my thanks to everyone who raised questions, contributed ideas, suggested resources, read and commented on drafts, and otherwise offered their wisdom for this project. This long list includes Sarah Albertson, Lori Anderson, Rev. Laura Peck Arico, Rev. Dr. Michelle Bartel, Tiffany Black, Jessica Ann Rouse Black, Dulcinea Boesenberg, Laure Elise Bourdages-Prévost, Kacy Brubaker, Rev. Dr. J. David Cassel, Charla Chailland, Paige Coulter-Kern, Lauren Croucher, Dr. Aimee Deiwert, Doug Denné, Justin Domingus, Bonnie Duffy, Peggy Duffy, Michelle Elder, Rev. Allison Rainey English, Brandon Feller, Jenny Gates, Alyson Goodwin, Abigail Fulton, Emily Hauguel, Erin Hougland, Katie Baker McDaniel, Annie Huey, Dr. Krista Hughes, Jahni Ittel, Dr. Kate Johnson, Tina Jones, Jessica Journey, Ashlee Kirk, Jeremy Koontz, Margaret Krantz, Kim Lude, Kim Lytle, Akami Marquis, Cerissa Marsh, Erin Duke McArdel, Dr. Sara Patterson, Rev. Dr. Barry Penn Hollar, David Austin Phelps, Carol Potochney, Katie Potochney, Dr. Chad Quaintance, W. Tania Rahman, Dr. David Reetz, Rev. Leah Robberts-Mosser, Zach Rotella, Mary Ruble, Dr. Robyn Ryle, Dr. Melanie

Shepherd, January Simpson, Nicole Smith Murphy, Rev. Katie Snipes Lancaster, Ariel Stewart, Glenda Stewart-Smythe, Jason Taber, Michelle Uhlenbrock, Melanie Votaw, Becky Voyles, Rev. Beth Walden, Brandiann Warren, Nick Waterfill, Katie Wood McPherson, and Rev. Dr. David Yeager.

I am blessed to be part of the Department of Theological Studies at Hanover. As part of our continuing support of one another's teaching and scholarship, we met on one occasion to discuss several of this book's early chapters. My colleagues' comments there, and on other chapters as their time allowed, improved this work. I am grateful to Krista Hughes and Sara Patterson for their encouragement and friendship. I am especially thankful to and for Dave Cassel, whose friendship has sustained me in countless ways for many years.

I want to thank Kacy Brubaker, Annie Huey, Tina Jones, Carol Potochney, and David Reetz for reading one or more drafts of one or more chapters and giving me important and helpful feedback.

I give special thanks to Laura Peck Arico, Kate Johnson, Ashlee Kirk, Margaret Krantz, and Sara Patterson, each of whom read a complete draft of the book. My deepest gratitude goes to Barry Penn Hollar and Becky Voyles, who suffered without complaint through the entirety of at least two full drafts. Barry's professional insights and faithful friendship continue to make me a better teacher, scholar, Christian, and person. Becky has been a healing presence and dear friend in my life for many years.

I am grateful to the Faculty Development Committee; the former Dean of Academic Affairs, Dr. Rob Graham; the President, Dr. Sue DeWine; and the Board of Trustees of Hanover College for approving the sabbatical that allowed me to write this book.

I am grateful to everyone at Westminster John Knox Press, including Daniel Braden, David Dobson, Robin Howell, Emily Kiefer, Nicole Smith Murphy (now at Baylor Press), Gavin Stephens, and Julie Tonini for helping to shepherd this book through the writing and publication process. My editor at WJK Press, Jana Riess, has been awesome. Her constant encouragement to bring this book out of its occasional intellectual cloudiness has greatly strengthened whatever connection the book might make with the reader. I appreciate her editorial work, and I am even more grateful for her personal support when writing became difficult.

I want to thank Rabbi Eugene Borowitz, Professor Harvey Cox, Professor Paul Mendes-Flohr, and especially Professor James F. Childress for all they have taught me about theology and ethics. No one should blame them for any mistakes of fact, reasoning, or imagination that I have made here.

My previous book was dedicated to my father, Donald Duffy; my sister, Peggy Duffy; and my late mother, Laura Tiemann Duffy. I am indebted to all three of them, now and always. This book is dedicated to my wife, Bonnie, whose tolerance of being a "book widow," as she calls it, astounds me, and whose love and laughter nourish and nurture me daily.

Introduction

Some years ago, I received a postcard from a friend. It was a photograph of a huge fireworks display; the other side contained only her name and return address and my mailing address. It took me just a few seconds to realize what she was telling me: she had just had sex for the first time. She had always been adamant about remaining a virgin until she was sure the "right person" came along. Now, well established in her career and planning her wedding, she believed she had found the right person and the right time. The fireworks card was her way of having a bit of fun with an important moment in her life.

"Fun" and "important" are two pretty good words with which to begin our exploration. Sex is fun. Under the right circumstances, it can be a delightful sharing of intimacy and pleasure with another person. It is a gift—from God or nature, however you want to think about it—that can unite us, make us laugh, give us joy, bring us a sense of peace, take us out of ourselves for a while, give us intense physical pleasure, allow us to give another person pleasure and delight, give us the opportunity to express and receive love, enhance our self-esteem, let us revel in touching and being touched, and help us to experience trust and vulnerability. Sometimes, it can even bring us the gift of children.

Sex is also important. Even in those admittedly too-frequent times when we choose to have sex under the wrong circumstances, so that we end up with more pain than pleasure, more sorrow than joy, sex is an important part of our lives. Sex brings together our intellectual, emotional, spiritual, and physical sides more clearly and intensely than most of the things we do. Our choices about whether, when, and with whom to participate in sexual activity define who we are in our eyes and others' eyes more deeply and readily than many other aspects of our behavior. Sex shapes the nature and quality of our relationships with certain other people, and from the point of view of those who believe in God, it can also shape the nature and quality of our relationship with God.

As enjoyable as sex can sometimes be and as important as the sexual dimension of our lives is, sex can also be complicated, and it is not unusual for us to find ourselves wondering whether and when to participate in it: Should I have sex with my girlfriend of three months? Should I hook up with this person I just met? Should my fiancé and I wait until we are married to have sex, or should we have it now? This book is intended to help you answer these kinds of questions for yourself. It is a book about how to make good sexual decisions, especially when those decisions involve sexual intercourse.

No Preaching Allowed Here

Let me promise you something: I am not going to preach to you. Over the last few years, I have had conversations with many current and past students, with Facebook friends and friends not on Facebook, and with colleagues and various professionals about what should be included in this book. Echoing through almost all of these conversations was one repeated request: Whatever issues you address, please don't tell us what to do or tell us what someone else wants us to do. Instead, write in a way that enables the reader to make up her or his own mind about the issues. I have tried to honor that request in this book. I am not going to try to tell you how to think or live. If you are looking for a book that will tell you what to do and what not to do and not challenge you to think for yourself, the book you are now holding is not for you. There are many people and resources that would be more than happy to tell you how to behave sexually; I am not one of those people, and this book is not such a resource. On the other hand, if you are looking for a book that, while taking an occasional stand on important issues, tries primarily to help you to think clearly and decide well about your own sexual life, I think you will enjoy the pages ahead.

Is This Book for Me If . . . ?

Is this book for me if I have already had sex? Definitely. After all, having sex before, whether once or a hundred times, does not mean that you need or want to have sex today. The decision is still yours to make, whether it is with a new person or with the same person as before. My goal here is not to convince you to start or to stop having sex, but simply to support you in making your own best decision.

Is this book for me if I am not single? Yes. The word "single" has at least two different meanings these days. It can refer to or describe those of us who are not married or not in a committed and intentionally lifelong relationship. It can also describe those of us who are not in any romantic relationship; some of my twenty-something friends would not consider themselves to be single if they had a boyfriend or girlfriend. In this book, I am using the word "single" in the first sense. Most anticipated readers will not be in committed, lifelong sexual relationships with their current partner. Yet many concerns related to sex and sexuality are not "solved" simply because one has made such a commitment, so I do think anyone can find it helpful to ponder the kinds of issues related to life and faith that this book addresses. You might also have siblings, children, grandchildren, nieces, nephews, and friends for whom these issues are currently or soon will be important, and it might be worth pondering some of these issues as you look for additional ways to support them.

Is this book for me if I am not of legal age? Yes and no. States have made judgments about when sex is and is not legal, and nothing I say here should be taken to encourage anyone to engage in illegal behaviors. In particular, I am not here to encourage anyone who is not of legal age to have sex. At the same time, even if you are younger than the intended audience for the book, you might find something in it that helps you to live your life well and think about your future; that seems to me to be a good thing.

Is this book for me if I am gay or lesbian? Yes and no. I do not believe that the mere fact that a sexual encounter or relationship is between people of the same gender is an argument against its appropriateness. You will find many of the issues here (about consent, caring for others, promises, motivations, and power, for instance) to be relevant to your process of sexual decision making no matter what your sexual orientation may be. At the same time, I have made the purely practical decision to focus the book on heterosexual vaginal intercourse and issues that emerge out of the heterosexual orientation with which I am experientially familiar.

Is this book for me whether or not I am a Christian? Yes. One of the things that must be considered as you ponder your sexual life is your faith tradition, if you have one, for it is likely to be the source of many of your values and ways of seeing the world. For that reason, and because my own faith commitment and the faith commitment of most of my expected readers is Christian, some of the discussions here will draw on the Christian tradition, and some are specifically designed to be matters of Christian discernment. At the same time, the majority of this book makes no reference to religious faith of any kind, and Christians and non-Christians alike can profit from its explorations. If we human beings are truly going to live together well and peacefully (and it is difficult to imagine any more worthwhile goal), then we must be able to talk together about common, key aspects of our lives. I hope to speak here a language that is common to as many of us as possible.

Is this book for me if I already know my answer to the question of whether I should have sex? Yes. Some of you know that you are not going to have sex until you are married, and some of you have decided that you are going to have sex whenever it is available. Yet, despite making some very firm decisions, many of you have reconsidered your decisions more than once. None of us knows what life is going to bring our way in the coming weeks and years. Since we can never truly consider ourselves to have decided much of anything "for all time," an attitude of continued openness to reflection seems most likely to help us to live well in a world where new insights, arguments, experiences, and innovations come our way frequently.

A Word about Me

I hope those quick questions and responses convinced you to keep reading. Perhaps a word about me is now in order. I am a white male whose sexual orientation and practice is and has been heterosexual. I was single for the first thirty-three years of my life, married for a decade, single for half a decade, in a committed relationship for a few years, and I am now married again. In my professional life, I spent thirteen years as pastor of a congregation and then as a college chaplain, and I have spent the last fifteen as a college faculty member. My interest in issues of sexuality has been both professional and personal; you can trust that I have addressed in my personal life, and as a pastor and teacher, the vast majority of the issues I am inviting you to address here. My continuing concern for our lived sexuality has led me to attempt the crazy feat of writing a book on sex.

As part of my promise not to preach to you, I am not going to say a lot in this book about my own views on sex. Instead, I am interested in giving you the tools to figure out what *you* think and how *you* choose to live. Just so you don't waste any time wondering whether I have a hidden agenda, though, let me say one thing: I believe sex can be morally appropriate inside and outside of marriage, and that it isn't *always* appropriate in either of those contexts. I will remind you of this later in the book.

Our Main Question and What It Means

This book's main question, stated from your point of view, is, "Should I have sex?" Two of the words in that question are especially important. The first word is "sex." In this question and most of the time in this book, the word "sex" refers to heterosexual vaginal intercourse. Many of the issues discussed here also illuminate other sexual practices, but intercourse in this sense is the sexual issue that comes up more than any other in my conversations with single twenty-somethings and is worth sustained attention. Indeed, focusing our attention in this way will enable us to make greater progress than if we were trying to cover a wider range of behaviors.

The second crucial word is "should." We use this word in a number of different ways. Compare what we mean when we say, "Should I use this fork for my salad?" and "Should I tell my friend the truth about his chances for getting this job?" Understood in a typical way, the first is the "should" of etiquette (e.g., what is the proper fork to use for salad in a formal eating situation?), and the second is the "should" of morality (e.g., is it right, or is it wrong, to treat another person in this way?). At the heart of this book is the *moral* question "Should I have sex?" To ask the same thing another way, "Is having sex in this situation the right way to treat the other person and the right way to treat myself?" Or, to be more formal, "Under what conditions is sexual intercourse morally justified?"

In a classroom setting, I can often feel the tension level rise when I start using terms such as "should," "morality," "justification," and the associated ideas and arguments. Such language makes us uncomfortable much of the time, as it is often used in both judgmental and divisive ways. This is not the aim of moral reflection, however. The aim of moral reflection is to help us to discern how to treat one another and ourselves as we struggle to live well and live together in this confusing and uncertain world. So when I use the shorthand question "Should I have sex?" I mean to be asking whether, in a holistic way (emotionally, physically, spiritually, intellectually), having sex in this situation (with this person, in this relationship, in this way, etc.) contributes to our well-being at least as well as any of the alternative actions open to us. To reflect on this question is part of what it means to aim to live a moral life.

I will sometimes write about sex being "morally appropriate" or "morally justified." To say something is morally *appropriate* is simply to say that it is, under these circumstances, a right thing to do. It may not be the *only* right thing to do (after all, you don't *have* to choose to have sex in a given situation), but it is right. It is, to use slightly more formal language, morally *permissible*. Similarly, to say something is morally *justified* simply means we can offer good reasons for doing it; it is a right action, and we can support it with reasons and arguments that would be generally accepted by rational, faithful, morally engaged people.

So in raising the question of whether to have sex, we are asking a question about the moral life and looking for good reasons and arguments to back up our response. Any two of us might well disagree on the answer, but if our reasons and arguments are well made, we will understand one another's position. In addition, where one of us is clearly being more rational and faithful than the other, the person with the poorer arguments may be led to change his or her mind. This process, of articulating and modeling the best moral position we can, continuing to explore other possibilities, and adjusting our point of view when better views are revealed, helps us to develop morally and spiritually and contributes to our living well and peacefully together.

Throughout this book, you will find that I speak of having sex as the result of a *decision*, even a rather complex one. You might disagree. After all, sex is often seen as something that "just happens." When sex *does* happen as the result of a decision, that decision often takes a few seconds or a few minutes, which is nowhere near enough time to read this book. The notion that sex is a more complex decision for some than for others certainly seems correct. I have spoken with people who spent many months thinking carefully about their religious traditions, their upbringing, and their personal values before having sex for the first time or with a new partner. I have also spoken with many whose participation in sex is much more spontaneous. I am assuming in this book that most of the time when we think carefully about moral issues, we end up acting more in accordance with our long-term well-being than when we act more spontaneously. I am assuming that quick moral decisions, just like other quick decisions in our lives, are more likely to be ones we regret and come to consider to have been wrong than those decisions to which we give more time and effort. If that assumption is correct, then, in the long run, spending some time thinking about our lives, including the question of whether we are going to have sex with some particular person, pays off for us and for others.

Puzzle Pieces

I remember sitting around my grandmother's kitchen table with her and other family members, decades ago, doing jigsaw puzzles. In a similar way, many of us, when faced with important life issues, spread the pieces out on a table in front of us in order to try to fit them together into a solution. Sometimes we do this metaphorically and sort through things in our heads, and sometimes we spread actual lists of pros and cons on the table in front of us and attempt to assemble them in a satisfactory way. One of the more complex puzzles we face as human beings is whether to have sex with a particular someone else. It is a complex puzzle because the physical, emotional, intellectual, and spiritual pieces can all swirl together to make the process both exciting and frustrating as we try to decide what we think, what we feel, and what we will do. Just as many people gathered around a table can contribute pieces to the jigsaw puzzle solution, we can factor into our sexual decisions the guidance, instruction, commands, demands, suggestions, and pleadings we receive from society, family, and peers. In the end, though, the group does not make the sexual decision; we must make up our own minds and take our best shot at a puzzle solution. I hope to illustrate, in the pages ahead, how we can solve the sometimes life-altering puzzle of whether to have sex, for the first time or the thousandth, in a random hookup or a committed relationship.

In the first section of this book, I will identify and explore ten puzzle pieces that can fit together in a number of different ways to answer the question of whether you should have sex. Each one of these pieces is many-sided, and the shape of each piece can change, quite unlike the pieces of a jigsaw puzzle, which are static and can fit together in only one way. The invention of the pill, for example, gave quite a different shape to considerations about birth control and its relevance to sexual behavior; this change in the birth-control piece meant this piece fit together differently with other pieces to yield, in the practice of many, a different puzzle solution. As another example, a decision you make about the absence or presence of God in your life might change the shape of one of your pieces in a way that changes your solution to the sexual puzzle. As you make the decision about whether to have sex, gain fresh insights, discover new innovations, come to understand your tradition in new or deeper ways, grow in your relationships, make new choices, or exercise your imagination, you may find puzzle pieces shifting shape and the puzzle having a different solution than it once had for you.

Once the ten pieces have been sorted and examined, and you have had an opportunity to decide where you stand on various dimensions of them, chapter 11 will sketch four different ways you might solve the puzzle. That there are more than four possibilities will be readily apparent to you, but these offerings will illustrate part of the process by which good sexual decisions can be made.

I have spoken about this book in some detail with perhaps a hundred people in the last couple of years. Many of them offered important questions to which I was simply unable to respond in the book's central chapters. At the end of the book, therefore, I have added my responses to what seem to me to have been the fifteen of those questions that were most frequently asked. In roughly a paragraph each, I will try to point to at least one way to think about the question and its answer.

Finally . . .

You will be invited to answer questions throughout this book. There are many of them in the text itself, and there are a few at the end of each chapter. They are part of my promise not to try to tell you what to do but to give you the resources to make good and healthy decisions for yourself. One of these resources is good questions. They are designed to help you to think about the puzzle and your solution of it. I encourage you not to skip over them. You may or may not answer every one, but you will find these pages much more rewarding and helpful if you ponder the ones that seem most applicable to you in your situation.

A large number of people have graciously allowed me to use stories from their lives, excerpts from interviews with them, and bits and pieces of their thoughts and feelings about sex for this book. All of them remain anonymous, and I have liberally changed identifying details without altering the heart of any quotation. In a few cases, typically identified as such, I have combined people and stories I have known into composites to make some point or other. The points are authentic, even if those few people and stories are to some extent invented.

By the end of this book, you should have a good sense of whether having sex is right or wrong for you at this time and with a given person. I will give you the puzzle pieces and some suggestions about how to put them together, but the final solution of the puzzle is up to you. I hope, in the pages that follow, to contribute positively and meaningfully to your sexual decision making. In the end, I am writing because I see confusion about sexual matters swirling all around us and the pain and anxiety that accompany this confusion; if I can do anything to add clarification to some issues and health to some relationships, I will be delighted.

PART 1   Puzzle Pieces
                          _____

Chapter 1

Informed Consent

What Do You Need to Know?

*T*ypically, when I ask a roomful of college students to name the conditions under which it is morally appropriate to have sex, the first word I hear is "consent." Given the number of nonconsensual sexual acts that occur on college campuses and in the wider society these days, this response may be a hopeful one, in that it suggests that students are taking to heart the message about consent that many colleges and universities are trying to convey. I will take for granted that mutual consent is a prerequisite for moral sex but, after sketching a few basic requirements of which most of you are aware, will invite you to consider a number of questions about what true consent looks like. In deciding whether to have sex, your first puzzle piece has these two parts:

1. A set of four nonnegotiable, if not absolutely precise, standards
2. The information, meanings, and awareness of life circumstances you need or want

Virtually Nonnegotiable Standards

To consent to something is to agree to it or to give permission for it. Of course, knowing this does not take us far, as we are immediately faced with the question of what constitutes agreement and permission. Does paying our taxes in full by April 15 entail our permission for local, state, and federal governments to use our tax money in whatever ways they wish? Does matriculating at a certain institution of higher learning mean that we agree to abide by any or all of its policies without complaint? Does being at the mall constitute permission for others to look at us and comment on what we are wearing, or must such permission be given in a different way? Such questions reveal a bit of the complexity of the issue of consent, and they do not have easy answers.

3

They do, however, have answers that have been agreed on to a significant extent by the relevant constituencies. Paying our taxes does entail permission to use them, but we have input into their use through voting and through our support of various elected officials. Matriculating at an institution of higher learning does mean we agree to abide by its policies, at least the ones with which we could be reasonably assumed to be familiar, but we also may work within the institution's structures to change those policies. Being in public does give some kind of permission for others to look at us, but they may not justifiably leer, ogle, insult, or respond to us in other defined ways. The question of whether others may comment on our appearance is one on which we perhaps have not reached a consensus, as "Nice hat!" and "Nice ass!" are quite different remarks and raise complicated issues of power. Aspects of these answers have been made into law.

Precisely what constitutes permission, agreement, or consent when it comes to sexual activity is at least as complex as the issues just mentioned. We have, as a society, reached a consensus on some broad principles, though the details of particular cases can make the broad consensus difficult to apply. In general, sexual activity is prohibited by law or by various institutional mandates and professional codes of ethics under these circumstances:

1. When someone is made to participate *unwillingly*
2. When one or both people are sufficiently *under the influence* of alcohol or drugs to make their consent problematic
3. When one or both people are judged to be *incompetent* to make decisions about having sex due to, for example, age or mental disability
4. When one person has *power over* another person in certain identifiable ways (professional, for instance)

It may be, as many people insist, that some of us can make perfectly competent decisions under the influence of certain amounts of alcohol. It may also be true, as some have argued, that sexual relationships between certain people who are not of the "age of consent" may sometimes, because of the maturity levels of the people involved, be morally acceptable (the fact that states disagree on the age of consent reflects differing views on this issue). And, certainly, there are many examples of "office romances" that have turned into flourishing and lasting relationships. So we may well want to give a *moral* assessment to *specific cases* of sexual activity such as those mentioned above that is different from a *legal* or *institutional* assessment. Do we, then, have any good reasons to adhere to the broad principles?

We do. These legal and institutional requirements are the result of tremendous amounts of societal stress, reflection, and debate. They are rightly considered to be both protecting the rights of individuals and supporting the common good. They protect others and us against the potent forces of self-deception (e.g., "I know I'm his professor and we had been drinking and he's underage, but we talked about it and decided we were both mature enough to have a sexual relationship"). These claims are too large to be defended in any depth here, but briefly consider the consequences of widespread rejection of any one of the four standards. What would such consequences be? I think you will agree that even such a quick evaluation reveals sufficient reasons to adhere to the basic standards as virtual absolutes.

Summary

The requirement of mutual consent expresses our deeply ingrained beliefs that each competent, adult human being ought to have an important, or even the final, say in what happens in her or his life. On the whole, we believe that, insofar as we are not harming anyone else, and with the occasional exception of laws made for the common good, our choices about what happens to us should override anyone else's choices about what happens to us. Simply by virtue of our personhood, then, sexual activity of any kind requires the consent of all parties involved. We have built this understanding into our legal and institutional systems in part by legislating that certain violations of the four requirements listed above may result in sexual assault charges. Specific aspects of these requirements are still under debate, but regarding them as virtually nonnegotiable will serve us well as the basis of our discussion of consent in sexual situations—and also as the basis of your first puzzle piece.

Other Dimensions of Consent—
What Do You Need to Know?

Even once we do our best to ensure that none of the four conditions given above will be violated if we have sex with someone, we still should think carefully about what it means to give consent. Suppose you sign a lease for an apartment. The lease includes a typical condition: "The owner of this apartment may, with twenty-four hours' notice to the renter, enter and inspect the apartment." By signing, you consent to this condition. After you have been in your new apartment for a week, you receive a call from the owner, who wants to inspect the apartment the next day. That seems odd to you, but you have agreed to the condition, so you make sure everything is neat, and the owner does a quick walk-through of the apartment. Less than a week later, he calls again, giving notice that he will be inspecting the apartment the following day. You soon realize that the owner is very particular about his apartment, and he plans to visit every few days. Your immediate response might well be, "I didn't know what I was getting into. I sure didn't agree to *this*."

And you would be right, sort of. You did not have all the information you needed to give your fully informed consent to the provisions in the lease. On the other hand, you did sign a lease that gave the owner permission to inspect the apartment with a day's notice. And this is all the owner did, even if he did it much more frequently than you expected. The bottom line here is that your consent was not *informed*.

Informed consent is an idea that is familiar to many of us through its role in medical settings. Before having surgery, for instance, we sign a consent form that describes, among other things, the risks attached to the surgery. Other things we may want to know before giving our consent include how many similar surgeries our doctor has done successfully and what the alternatives to the surgery might be. But the significance of informed consent goes well beyond its medical use to virtually any situation in which we are asked to agree to anything. A friend of mine realized this when he called his father to get advice about negotiating the terms of his first job offer. His father told him to ask questions about salary, pension contributions, health insurance, vacation days, supervisory structures, and a number of other things. Later, my friend noted that the conversation with his father enabled him to make his job decision a truly informed one.

The best time to become informed is before the actual moment of signing for the apartment or agreeing to a surgical procedure or accepting a job. This is also true about our sexual decisions; we gather the information beforehand so that we can make informed decisions when the time comes. There is, however, one important way in which these examples differ, and we should keep it in mind in our exploration. Typically, when we rent an apartment, we sign a contract binding us to a particular set of responsibilities. Consent, in such cases, is given once; after that, we are legally and morally obligated to follow the terms of the contract. When we consent to surgery or accept a job, we also sign an agreement, though these situations may come with greater flexibility than the rental situation, should we change our minds. Sexual consent does not come with a written contract, and it is highly susceptible to being withdrawn. At any point, one partner or the other may simply take back his or her consent, and that legally and morally ends the sexual encounter. We should remember as we go that sexual consent is not a one-time agreement but must be maintained throughout any sexual encounter or relationship. With that caveat in mind, the remainder of this chapter invites you to think about what you need to know before you consent or continue to consent to having sex with someone.

In addition to our four basic principles, there are at least three areas where the role of informed consent in our sexual lives calls for some careful reflection and decision making. I will call these areas *information, meanings*, and *self-awareness*. These dimensions of sexual decisions are less frequently discussed than the earlier four components, yet I suspect they are more relevant to most of us in the circumstances in which we typically make our decisions. To kick off our discussion of them, here's a situation to ponder:

> Nineteen-year-old Melinda has known nineteen-year-old John for a month. They see each other in an economics class three times every week, they have lunch together about once a week, and they have run into each other at weekend parties three or four times, where they have enjoyed talking and dancing. One night, they are dancing at a party at which neither has been drinking, and Melinda asks John if he wants to go back to her room. He says yes. Once there, they begin kissing enthusiastically and slowly undress one another. John asks Melinda if she wants to have sex, and she says yes. John puts on a condom, and John and Melinda have sex.

Let's stipulate that Melinda and John are acting in accordance with the four basic principles. How, if at all, might differences in information, meanings, and self-awareness have altered their decision? How should we account for these differences in our sexual encounters and relationships? What do you need to know about yourself and another person in order to give your informed consent to having sex with her or him? Answering these kinds of questions will give you the shape of the flexible parts of this puzzle piece as you assemble your solution.

Knowing Information

Suppose John has a girlfriend. Would Melinda want to know? Would you, in her place? Suppose Melinda had unprotected sex recently. Would John want to know? Would you, in his place? Would you be consenting to sex if you did not know these things? As with the beleaguered renter mentioned above, the answer is probably yes and no. You would be consenting by saying yes to sex. But since you did not know all the relevant information, your consent would not be informed; you did not consent to having sex with someone who is otherwise involved or someone who had unprotected sex recently. Or, to say it another way, you did not *truly* or *fully* consent.

Much of the information we might want to know in order to consent fully is more future oriented than the examples just mentioned. For instance, what if, a year after the events described in the scenario and some months after John and Melinda have decided that they want to "just be friends" and want not to have sex any more, John meets and falls in love with Cindy? The first time John and Cindy discuss any kind of sexual activity, John reveals his prior sexual relationship with Melinda. Cindy ends the romance at this point, as she has been "saving herself" for marriage and wants to marry someone who is also a virgin. John is devastated.

I can imagine some of you thinking that Cindy is crazy and that John is better off without her. Others might say John got what he deserved for being promiscuous with Melinda. Some will rightly note that being "devastated" can be a consequence of good decisions as well as bad ones, so the mere fact that John has a difficult time with Cindy's decision does not mean he was wrong to have sex with Melinda. And a few of you might suppose there is no such person as Cindy, since you don't personally know anyone like her. But the situation is not so unusual. There are many young men and women these days who believe, for instance, that God has one particular person picked out for them to marry. They are "saving themselves" for that person and expect that person to be doing the same. Indeed, a young woman walked into my office not long ago, unable to shake a feeling of jealousy and anger over her boyfriend's previous sexual experiences. He was technically still a virgin, she said, but he had been sexually active in other ways, with two different women, and this really bothered her. She and her boyfriend worked through this difficulty and remained together, but that conclusion was not a given at the time we talked. I mention this situation simply to note that Cindy's expectation is not unreal. I hear many young adults expressing something very like Cindy's approach to life. This notion of waiting or being waited for is very important to some people. What do we do with the uncertainty of meeting and falling in love with one of them? How should we live sexually when we don't know what the future will bring?

Consider some other possibilities for the future of John and Melinda's relationship. We can imagine them, a week after their sexual encounter, feeling a bit embarrassed, laughing with one another and going on with their friendship, saying, "*That's* never going to happen again!" Or, we can imagine them alienated from one another and wishing the sex had never happened. We can also imagine them falling deeply in love and living happily ever after. In having sex, John and Melinda were not, we may assume, aware of these possibilities attendant upon their decisions. They may well not have been thinking about tomorrow or next year at all. How do we evaluate unattainable information from the future when we think about having sex today? Is our contemplated sexual encounter important enough to override the possibility of falling in love with someone tomorrow who cannot deal with what we have done? Is having sex tonight or with this person worth the possibility that the sex will contribute to loving or hating one another tomorrow? This is a situation John and Melinda face, even if they do not think about it, when they decide to have sex after the party. There is some information we simply do not and cannot know when we live life forward, which, of course, is the only direction in which it can be lived. How, then, should we live? How will *you* live?

Meanings

The next dimension of the puzzle piece of consent is the differing meanings that people often give to or see in the same event. One of my many college roommates was not opposed to an occasional one-night stand. A couple of weeks after one of these nights, the woman involved, who had been visiting the college to see whether she wanted to attend, called him to say that she wanted to stay in touch. I remember him yelling when he got off the phone, "Why does sex have to *mean* anything? Why can't two people just screw?" Some of you will say "Amen" to his protestations, and some of you will think he was a jerk, but whatever else may be true, he and his partner clearly had different understandings of what their night together meant and of what they wanted it to mean.

Here is an elaboration of our Melinda-John scenario that might help us ponder all this.

> Melinda has been involved in fairly intense levels of sexual activity since she was sixteen and has always considered it a way to have fun and feel good with special friends. She has slept with five or six different people in these three years. John, on the other hand, has never had a girlfriend and has seen sex as something you wait to do at least until you are in a steady relationship, which is the way he now sees his friendship with Melinda. Melinda is looking forward to a night of pleasure with her hot new friend, John; John is looking forward to a night of bonding; and neither is particularly aware of these differences as they are making out and getting naked.

Again, Melinda and John are agreeing to have sex, and neither one of them is being coerced. In the most basic sense, this is consensual sex. What is fascinating, however, is that Melinda and John are consenting to different things. John is consenting to sharing love with Melinda, with whom he is, he believes, in a new and steady relationship. Melinda is consenting to sharing orgasm with John, whom she considers to be a new friend, but she would be appalled to think they were about to "make love." Notice, also, that these differences in meaning might not be apparent to either John or Melinda without some explicit discussion of them, especially when they are in a state of arousal. It could well be the case that neither John nor Melinda could discern the meaning of their activity to the other person through anything that happens during their night of passion. Would either of them still consent to have sex if she or he knew that the other person's view of the meaning of the sexual sharing differed from hers or his? What do *you* want to have figured out about the meaning of sex in general or of a particular sexual encounter, to yourself and to your possible partner, before having sex?

Self-Awareness

In addition to questions of information and meaning, our awareness of what has happened or is happening in our lives that might push us toward or away from having sex with a given person at a given time is important. We will look at the intertwined issue of reasons for having sex in chapter 8, but even at this early stage in our exploration, it's worth pondering a few of the life occurrences that might shape our choice to have sex or not to have it. Consider the relevance of the following situations to John and Melinda's encounter.

- Melinda was just dumped by a long-term boyfriend she believed to be the one love of her life.
- John's parents never showed him any love or support, creating an emptiness that has conditioned much of his life.
- John's friends tease him constantly about being a virgin, and he is hungry for their acceptance.
- Melinda's grandfather, who lives two thousand miles away, has just been taken to the hospital and may not make it through the night.

A decision to have sex in these kinds of situations may not be plagued by a lack of information or a difference between the two people about the meaning of the experience; rather, the issue here may be self-awareness. If you were Melinda, perhaps you would still have sex with John if you were aware that you wanted to soothe the ache inside you caused by missing the love of your life or alleviate your despair over your beloved grandfather's health. Perhaps, if you were John, you would still have sex with Melinda, all the while aware that you were succumbing to the persecution of being teased as a virgin or trying to fill the emptiness inside of you because of your parents' emotional distance. You might, on the other hand, decide not to have sex if you were aware of the depths of these wounds and realized they were likely to lead you to do things you would regret later. Many of the deep emotional influences on our actions remain hidden from us. We still consent to act, but we do so without full awareness of the ways we are being influenced. If any of these were true, would your view of whether John and Melinda's sexual activity was smart or not smart, or right or wrong, or consensual or not, be changed? Are there situations in your own life that might lead you toward or away from sex that you have not pondered?

Conclusion

An hour spent discussing information, meanings, and life events might dampen or enhance sexual attraction. Two people might find themselves much more interested or much less interested in having sex together after an hour of talking about it. Yet this is the point to which each of our first two discussions, on information and meanings, leads us. The only way John can know whether Melinda is on the pill is to ask her. The only way Melinda can know what sex means to John is to ask him. Communication about such things is important to the quality and the consequences of the sexual encounter or relationship.

Awareness of the situations in our lives that lead us toward or away from sex may or may not require conversation with our prospective partners, but it does require some reflection of our own, reflection I hope this book will encourage. Indeed, information and meanings also have a self-awareness component: we need to become aware of what we each need to know in order to have sex with another person, and we each need to know what sex means to us in order to have sex with another person. Without awareness of these issues, we become likely to do things that we either later regard as wrong or that we later regret. Why do *that* to ourselves? Sexual pleasure is a great good, but I don't think its pursuit and attainment are worth every possible cost. What do you think?

Our initial scenario with John and Melinda appears to present a case of consensual sex, not just legally but morally as well. Some would argue that two unmarried people having casual sex is immoral, or that two people not in a long-term relationship should not be having sex, but most people looking at this case would not, it seems to me, judge the sex to be wrong on the basis of nonconsensuality. Two adults decide together to have sex, having talked about it to at least some extent, and they do so willingly as far as we can tell. If unmarried sex can be moral with mutual consent, this seems like one of those cases.

What we cannot tell from looking at the scenario, however, is to what extent Melinda and John may be *informed* about the information, meanings, and life situations that are relevant to their decision and action. Of course, having sex without being aware of every possible risk and benefit is not immoral; this is the way we always have sex. Likewise, we are never aware of every emotional or psychological pressure that influences us to have sex or not to have it. To say that complete awareness is required for true consent would be saying, in effect, that no human being consents, morally speaking, to much of anything in this life and so acts or is acted on immorally on many occasions. We never fully understand the possible consequences of our actions, and we are always shaped in our moral choices by hidden realities. Yet, as with surgeries and apartment leasing and accepting jobs, some level of awareness of information, meanings, and life situations seems crucial to our ability to make good decisions. It would be wrong, I think we would agree, for a surgeon to perform a surgery without telling a fully conscious and competent patient what part of the body she was planning on removing; that's an important bit of information! It would be immoral to rent an apartment to someone without telling him that there is an irremediable roach problem in his bedroom. It would seem to be at least a very poor decision to have sex with someone without finding out whether he or she has a sexually transmitted infection (STI), and it might well be deceptive to have sex with someone if we just want to have an orgasm and we don't know whether our partner is in love with us. But this kind of information only comes our way through conversation. It is self-reflection followed by honest communication that remedies problems of lack of awareness about relevant information and differences in meaning.

Finally, note that there is a level of trust necessary for this kind of communication. If we do not know whether we can trust our prospective partner to be honest in response to the concerns we express or the questions we ask, then we might well decide to hold off on sex unless and until the situation changes. If, for instance, we are not sure we can trust our partner to tell us whether he or she has been cheating on us, we might think twice about having sex with him or her. Of course, if we are not trustworthy enough ourselves to be honest in telling our partner what he or she needs to know in order to consent fully to having sex with us, then we also might want to think twice about having sex, for we are depriving our partner of an aspect of his or her humanity. This offers a final bit of reflection for our exploration of consent: Do you trust your prospective partner to be honest with you in response to whatever questions you decide you need answered before having sex with her or him? Are you trustworthy enough to answer your partner's questions truthfully? How does your trust or lack of it, or trustworthiness or lack of it, contribute to your decision about whether to have sex?

Promoting awareness of the importance of consent in sexual relationships is crucial as one way of trying to prevent situations in which someone is coerced against her or his will into having sex. We want to be sure, in one of the most vulnerable areas of human life, that people are able to do what they really want to do. As our exploration has suggested, however, this notion of what we *really* want is a tricky one. We all consent to many things without full information and without clearheadedness. That's the way life must be. Yet as we seek to live well, each one of us must ask herself or himself how much information and self-understanding is sufficient to let us know that we are acting rightly and doing good. So where do you think the moral lines should be drawn here? How do you want to shape this consent puzzle piece in order to make it best contribute to your overall decision about having sex? How much and what do *you* need to know in order to have sex?

Questions for Reflection and Discussion

1. If there are points of view in this chapter with which you disagree, how would you argue your own opposing view?
2. If you want to have sex and someone tells you no, then you cannot have sex with that person: no means no. If you want to have sex and someone tells you yes, would it always be appropriate to have sex with him or her? Is every yes a yes? Is a reluctant yes consent?
3. What do you need to know from or about your partner in order to have sex? Why is your list of what you need to know a good list for you?
4. At least at this moment, what does sex mean to you?
5. For you, to what extent are the need for information, the understanding of meanings, and the awareness of relevant life circumstances important for nonintercourse sexual activity? Consider kissing and oral sex, for instance.
6. What are the most important life circumstances that are currently shaping your thinking and feeling about having sex? What impact does your awareness have on what you will do?

Chapter 2

How Do You Want to Treat Other People?

*I*n the previous chapter, I invited you to think about what it means to consent fully to sex, and the focus of the chapter was on becoming aware of things in your own life that might help or hinder that consent. Although what we said there implies being sure that any sexual partners we have are also fully consenting, in this current chapter, we begin to turn outward more explicitly. Our focus here is on how we want to treat other people in our lives. Among these other people, of course, are our possible or actual sexual partners, and we will pay special attention to how we should treat them.

There are four basic ways to treat others. The first is to *watch out for number one*. In essence, this means that we take no responsibility for what others want or need and focus on what we want and need. In real life, this probably comes in two versions: watch out for number one *only* and, alternatively, watch out for number one *first*. This leads to the second basic way of treating others: *Do no harm*. In this approach, we accept responsibility not to make other people's lives (or our own lives) worse. The third basic approach says that not only will we not make the lives of others worse, but we will *foster good* in others' lives. When we choose to live in this way, we accept some responsibility for trying to make other people's lives better. The fourth and final approach is typically associated with religious traditions. In adopting it as a guideline for life, we accept responsibility to *love the neighbor*. This begins with fostering good and adds an element of self-sacrifice to it. When we choose not only to foster good but also to love our neighbor, we choose to try to make others' lives better, even at some significant risk or cost to ourselves. The third and fourth approaches tend to accompany a worldview that sees our lives as being more intimately tied to one another than the first two approaches. Let's look at these four views in order.

15

Watching Out for Number One

In response to any suggestion that it might be important to care about things such as whether my partner understands the meaning of sex differently than I do, I sometimes hear a comment like this:

> Look, I'm not responsible for everyone else. We are each responsible for ourselves. It's not my job to ponder why my sexual partner is agreeing to have sex with me. That's crazy. I watch out for myself in these things, and I expect other people to do the same.

As far I can tell, these sentiments are not rare. Some of us are always ready to claim that our task is to take care of ourselves and not to worry about what our potential or actual sexual partners are thinking or doing. Sometimes we mean quite literally that people should not concern themselves with things like whether a partner is making a good sexual decision or a bad one, or whether she or he will regret things in the morning. We should instead, so this view holds, be concerned only with whether *we* will be okay in the morning. If we apply this view to our scenario from the previous chapter, John's view of what sex means would not be Melinda's concern and whether Melinda is in an unusually vulnerable place in her life would not be John's concern. Except for a basic respect for the four fundamental principles of consent we listed in chapter 1, this view would have us say to one another, *Your issues are not my issues, and I will just assume you know what you are getting into.*

Most of us do not hold this view as a considered position, though more than a few of us probably act as though it is our guideline for life at least some of the time. Mostly, we show some level of positive concern for what other people are going through in their lives, a concern that extends to sexual encounters and relationships. But sex seems to be one of those places where the "Watch out for number one only" approach can easily take over. The pull of sexual energy is very strong; our considered points of view can easily be overcome in aroused moments; and it is ridiculously easy to have sex now and ask questions, even of ourselves, later. Here, from a longtime friend of mine, is a crude example of how the desire for sex led someone to think only about himself.

> Many years ago, when I was in college, I lived in a suite with a bunch of guys. One weekend, one of my suitemates had a friend visiting from another college. Late at night, when several of us were sitting around watching TV, the friend (I'll call him Martin) stuck his head in the suite door and whispered something like this: "Guys, don't laugh. I know this

girl isn't very pretty, but she's the one I could get to come back with me. Just don't say anything." He then opened the door wide and ushered in a young woman; they walked into my suitemate's room and closed the door. None of us laughed; I remember just thinking what an ass this guy was. When a couple of us ran into Martin the next day, he said how awful it was to see the young woman sitting on the edge of the bed in the morning, just staring out the window and obviously hurting. "I hate it when they do that," he commented.

We can be thankful that few people would support Martin's activity as a considered position. But, again, that's not to say that we have never acted in a similar way, whether in a sexual situation or not.

The "Watch out for number one only" position should not be confused with a position that also advocates watching out for number one but leaves off the "only." Sometimes looking out for number one has the meaning of taking good care of ourselves, and it can simply reflect the recognition that we are often our own best advocates in the world, who cannot expect anyone else to protect us from the consequences of our bad choices. This may or may not describe the world in which many of us would like to live, but it does describe the way the world often is. In this sense, without the "only," it seems as though most of us would accept looking out for number one as a helpful reminder of our responsibility to ourselves, in our sexual activity and elsewhere.

Pause for a moment to reflect on this first approach. That will enable you to be better prepared to evaluate the following section. What do you think of "Watch out for number one only" as a guideline for your life, sexually or otherwise? Most of you will interact with other people before the day is over, and some of you may be sexually active today. Is our first approach the shape this puzzle piece will take for you?

Do No Harm

A second possible shape for the puzzle piece of how we should treat one another is captured in the traditional principle that we should do no harm. We Americans have been imbued with the sense that we can do what we want unless it is harmful to other people. If asked what is morally right and wrong, many of us will say something like this: "Morality is a matter of personal choice, and you should be able to do whatever you want to do, as long as you're not actually harming anyone else." In our political traditions, not harming others without providing convincing reasons is considered a fundamental principle of a civilized society. Therefore, it is easy to find complex legal and moral analyses of the meaning of harm and principles of harm. Here, though, all I want to call to mind is our basic insight that, somehow or other, the ways we choose to act should be limited at the point of their negative effect on others. We should, most of us think, be able to kiss whomever we want to kiss, fondle whomever we want to fondle, and have sex with whomever we want, as long as we are not causing them harm, affecting them negatively, or impinging on their legitimate interest in defining their own chosen life.

It is important to remember, but easy to forget, that each of us is among those we should not harm. The harm principle does not distinguish among people. It says that we may not harm people without strong, justifying reasons. (An extended version of the principle could include nonhuman life forms, the environment, or even the entire cosmos among those things we should not harm, but I am restricting this discussion to human beings.) When we adopt it as our guideline for living or for sex, we do so with the recognition that we may not harm ourselves any more than we may harm another person. For example, if someone wishes to kiss us, we only allow this if we are not harmed in the process.

On the face of it, this point seems pretty obvious. Human nature being what it is, it seems unlikely that we would accept the view that people should not be harmed but then turn around and harm ourselves. However unlikely it seems, however, we hear about it all the time. I remember a friend in college reporting on her previous night's date: "He bought me dinner; the least I could do was have sex with him." I remember her being a very kind person, certainly one who never wanted to harm others but who clearly was willing to act in ways that devalued herself. The problem was not that she had sex with her date—we might assess that in any number of ways, as I hope this book makes clear—but that she only had sex so as not to hurt her date's feelings. She valued giving herself to him sexually (her understanding when she spoke of it in other circumstances was that having sex involved "giving herself") the same as she valued being bought dinner. Rather than a high valuing of the dinner, this was a devaluing of herself. We could, I expect, offer all kinds of examples of ways in which people who live by the "Do no harm" code do not include themselves among those who should be valued, a mistake we should be sure not to make in our own reasoning.

One of the significant ways the harm principle is relevant to sexual encounters or relationships concerns the spread of sexually transmitted infections (STIs). You may have heard more than you ever want to hear about these infections, but not spreading them is an important way for us not to harm our sexual partners, so let's spend a moment reflecting on them. At the end of this chapter, I'll offer a question you might use to continue your reflections, but here is an example from my graduate student career that highlights potential relational harms.

> At one point in my long educational journey, I was walking through the campus center of the university I was attending when I ran into a friend. I hadn't seen him in a while and stopped to chat with him. When I asked him how he was doing, he responded, "I'm hurting, man; you need to buy me a drink." We went to get a drink, and he told me he had just had two shots of penicillin in his butt because he had contracted syphilis from someone. It turns out there were eight or ten people it might have been, and he now needed to call them all and tell them to be tested and treated. Many of these were not especially pleasant phone calls.

It's difficult to know all of the specific harms that might be part of this situation. I don't know, for instance, whether one or more of the people involved might have been infected long enough to have suffered the health complications that may accompany untreated syphilis. I do know, given another chat with my friend a few months later, that friendships were harmed, as anger and suspicion were tossed around: Who gave what to whom, and who should have been more responsible, and who knew what but didn't tell? In the end, the answers to the questions almost don't matter, as trust once lost is difficult to regain. Nor does it matter who was in the right or who was in the wrong; human relationships are fragile things, often harmed whether it makes rational sense or not. Even relatively easily treated STIs may be accompanied by great harm at the level of personal relationships.

Let's leave this section by raising some final questions. As you ponder to what extent your guideline for treating other people will be not to harm them, how do you understand the role of this guideline in sexual encounters or relationships? It seems clear that we are harming someone if we know we have an STI but fail to tell our partner this before we have sex. Are we also harming someone if we aren't sure whether we have an STI because, say, we have had unprotected sex recently, but we do not disclose this? Is putting someone at risk of harm essentially the same as harming her or him? Drawing on our previous chapter, it is certainly the case that we harm someone if we become sexual with her or him without consent. Is it also harmful if we fail to be sure our partner is as fully consenting as possible? For instance, is it harmful not to explain what sex means to us and ask them to do the same? In the next section, we will look at what happens if we raise the level of responsibility up a notch or two beyond the commitment not to harm.

Foster Good

Fostering good is the third shape this puzzle piece might take. Typically, this principle is built on top of the foundation of doing no harm. We choose to go beyond not doing anything that is directly harmful to other people and, in addition, act in ways that contribute positively to their lives. Let's look at a situation that has nothing to do with sex, but should help us think about the important differences between these two guidelines for treating others.

Imagine you are walking along a sidewalk in your neighborhood on a hot day and you see a small toddler splashing around and having fun in a wading pool in her front yard, just a few feet from the sidewalk. Suddenly, the toddler slips, falls, and slides under the water. Do you have a responsibility to help the toddler? In my experience, the vast majority of people say yes. If all you need to do is take two steps, reach down and pull the toddler to safety, or if all you need to do is yell to the mother who is three feet away but distracted by another child for a moment, and you do not do it, then, in the eyes of most people, you have done something wrong. You have not lived up to your moral responsibility as a human being.

At the same time, however, you did not directly harm the child. You did not kick the toddler's feet out from under her, and you did not try to hold her head under the water. You could have stood on the sidewalk and done nothing, and you would have satisfied the condition of not directly harming someone. Most people will think you did something wrong, but you did not necessarily violate the "Do no harm" principle. Instead, you failed to do the positively good act of helping the child.

Of course, our expectations of you would change if we added sufficient risks to the situation. If there were a minefield between you and the wading pool, or if the pool were very deep and you could not swim, we might think differently. We would probably still think you had *some kind* of responsibility (to yell for help, for instance), but we would normally think your direct responsibility to aid varies inversely with the amount of risk involved: the greater your risk, the less your responsibility. Consider it this way: One of the reasons no one condemns us for not making a trip to the nearest hospital to be tissue-typed, so that we can contribute a kidney to someone who might well die without our contribution, is that most of us consider the cost to be too high in this case. Again, one of the reasons we are unlikely to stop and help someone whose car is broken down alongside the road or interrupt our schedule to take the next homeless person we meet to lunch is that we consider these things to have potentially high costs or risks. On the other hand, many people consider giving blood to be almost a moral responsibility; if there were no needle stick involved, it might seem even more so. Most seem to think that giving unneeded money to someone who needs it is something we should do. Many consider calling the local police or sheriff to inform them of the broken-down traveler a near-duty. The less cost or risk we build into the situation, the more it ascends to the level of moral requirement.

How are you thinking about your sex life at this point? Will you act only for yourself? Will you choose to live so as not to be directly harmful to others? Will you choose to foster good in the world, at least as long as the risks to you are not too great? Will you live by one of these in certain areas of your life and another one in another area? Where do you stand at this point?

In a situation such as the John-Melinda scenario in the previous chapter, what might it mean to foster good? If not harming means refraining from doing anything that would harm the other person, and fostering good means actively doing things that will benefit the other person, then we could spend a lot of time wrestling with what it means to refrain and what it means to foster, but let's not do that. Instead, let's stick with what would appear to be a couple of obvious points, given our discussion so far. Not to harm means, for instance, not to have sex with someone when we know we have an STI and, if we are not going to harm ourselves, being sure the other person does not have one as well. Not to harm means not having sex without the other person's consent and being sure we are as fully consenting as possible. Not to harm means not having sex when we know that the encounter means something very different to each one of us and we have not discussed this. Fostering good is a higher level of responsibility and calls for a bit more work on our part. It is likely to mean added communication between partners, for instance, as doing good for Melinda might require John to know that Melinda's grandfather has just gone into the hospital. He might offer to talk with her rather than having sex with her. Fostering good might require Melinda to know a bit about John's home situation or peer pressures, so that she can support him in dealing with the real issues in his life, rather than simply giving him a few moments of sexual gratification.

This is not to say that fostering good precludes having sex; it certainly does not. Sex can be a way of showing love for another person, of nurturing and supporting him or her, especially in a context where the sex is surrounded by other forms of caring, including conversation. It can bring great pleasure, moments of bonding and soothing, a uniting not easy to find outside of the sexual experience. Having sex can be "making love," in a very literal way, which is surely a fostering of good. Sex always occurs in the midst of some particular set of circumstances, and we need to understand these in order to know, as far as we can, whether having sex or not having sex would promote the greatest good.

You may well be thinking that this is all just ridiculous and unrealistic. Who is going to stop in the heat of passionate embraces and sexual arousal to ponder the emotional and spiritual life of their partner? If he or she wants to keep going, we often think, then I am going to keep going! Remember, though, we are not talking here about what we may want to do or will do in the heat of the moment; we are talking about what we believe we *should* do when we are away from the immediate desire to have sex and are determined to make thoughtful choices about how we want to live our lives, sexually speaking. So, what do you think: Will your sexual life be about not harming others, fostering good in their lives, or will it be about our next possible shape for this puzzle piece, loving our neighbors?

Love Your Neighbor as Yourself

There is yet another shape that this puzzle piece might take. As hinted at in the previous section, if we add to the notion that we should foster good in others' lives the imperative to do this *even at significant cost to ourselves*, we get something like the "Love your neighbor as yourself" principle. While most of us are familiar with this through the New Testament, versions of it are found in the Old Testament and in the world's major religious traditions, and it also has non-religious counterparts. The claim here is not only that I should not harm the other person and not only that I should foster good for them, but also that I should foster good in a particular way.

In the Christian context, one model for loving the neighbor in this way is the well-known Good Samaritan parable, found in the Gospel of Luke (10:25–37). Ways of engaging this story abound, but the basic point is clear. Several people, who might be abiding by the principle to do no harm, walk by the wounded man. A man from a reviled culture comes by and risks his reputation, his time, his money, his energy, and quite possibly his own physical well-being to help. He is not only living out of a principle of fostering good, but out of a principle of fostering good for a person in need at significant cost to himself. This is one way to understand what it means to love one's neighbor. He might have lessened the risk to himself and still fostered good: he might have given the injured man some bandages, for instance, or left some money with him to pay for help when someone else came by. He might have ridden to get help from others. But he chose to take the cost of helping on himself.

But how is this loving the neighbor "as yourself," which is the language Jesus uses? Isn't the Samaritan *not* loving himself when he puts himself at risk for the sake of another person? There is certainly some ambiguity in the "as yourself" language here, but there's no need to get hung up on it. We can simply read that clause as something similar to what we noted with previous principles. I am one of the people not to be harmed. I am one of the people whose good should be fostered. And I am one of the people to be loved. In adopting any of these guidelines for life, we include ourselves among those not to be harmed and to be cared for. How many times in life do we give up one good thing in order to obtain another good thing—money and time for better health, for example?

What would it mean to go out of one's way, to accept some cost to oneself, for the overall well-being of a prospective sexual partner? It might mean paying attention to him or her as a whole person and not just a sexual object. It might mean putting extra time and energy into learning what makes one's partner happy in life and what satisfies her or him sexually. It might mean not having sex, even though we really want to, when we have even a slight reason to believe it is not in the other person's best interest. It might mean waiting for sex, even in the presence of lots of sexual energy between us, until other dimensions of our relationship are established.

Consider where you are in sorting out this sexual puzzle of whether to have sex with a given partner in the circumstances of your life. What would it mean to adopt one of the four guidelines offered here as your way of treating that partner? What would it mean to adopt one of them as your overall way of life? How would you live similarly to or differently from the way you now live?

How Will You Treat Relationships?

In the next chapter, we are going to ask in what kind of relationship we want to be when we have sex. Perhaps it is reasonable for two people who are strangers to one another to have sex. Maybe we should be open to having sex with our friends. Perhaps a long-term, even if not permanent, relationship seems reasonable and sufficient for us, or we might be among those who are waiting to be married before having sex. Before we take up these issues, let's address one additional issue in this chapter. It is not only other people that we choose to treat in one way or another; relationships themselves may also be loved, sacrificed for, harmed or not harmed, nurtured or not nurtured. Along with our questions about how we will treat others are questions about how we will treat our relationships.

We owe a debt of gratitude to the environmental movement for reminding us that our actions impinge upon one another's lives in seen and unseen ways. Each one of us is in some kind of relationship with every other one of us. Whether we are friends, enemies, lovers, spouses, coworkers, physicians and patients, personal trainers and clients, parents and children, siblings, citizens of the same planet, or several of these at the same time, we are in many ways defined by our relationships. Each of our relationships can be harmed or enhanced, and how we choose to treat them will end up defining a significant part of our lives, whether we wish it to or not. One of the invitations this book offers is to look at the relationships in which we might have or are having sex and consciously and carefully ask how we will treat them.

Here is how one person (let's call her Megan) describes part of her thought process when she is deciding whether to have sex with someone.

> So, when I consider whether or not to have sexual relations with a partner now [I ask myself questions such as,] Would entering into consensual relations potentially harm our relationship or our relationships with others? How might having a sexual relationship deepen and help our relationship grow?

Megan is clear about the focus of her sexual decision making: the relationship she has with the prospective partner. She tries to discern whether having sex with someone, whether the person is a stranger she has just met or someone she has been dating for months, will "deepen and help" their relationship or "harm it." It is, of course, impossible to know the answer for sure. Maybe sex will distract Megan and her partner from a new friendship and focus them only on the pursuit of physical pleasure. Maybe it will take a growing and deepening friendship and add a dimension of physical nurturing to it. Perhaps all we know for sure is that adding sex or not adding sex into any relationship will change that relationship in some way or other, even if that change is minuscule. As someone pondering how you will live sexually, attempting to discern what is or is not best for the relationship you are in or pondering becomes an important task.

The question of how we should treat one another is a significant moral question, and the answer impinges upon many more issues than the sexual ones that are our current focus. But the bottom line here is this: You are going to treat others, including those who might be or currently are your sexual partners, in some way or other, and you are going to allow yourself to be treated in some way or other. Are you determined not to harm others in any way? Do you want to love others even to the point of significant cost to yourself? As you explore these and the other options in this chapter and construct your own approach, you will have your second puzzle piece.

Questions for Reflection and Discussion

1. Do you believe it is important for you and your prospective partner to be on the same page in your answer to the question of how you treat one another or your relationship? Why or why not?
2. In what way does the prevalence of STIs affect your sexual practices? Check out cdc.gov for current information about chlamydia, HPV, herpes, and HIV. Currently, an HPV shot is being developed for males. If you are male, will you have it when it's ready? If you are female, will you ask your partner whether he has had it?
3. How is the kind of love discussed in this chapter like or unlike other ways of thinking about love?
4. Are you likely to treat different people in your life according to different principles? Do you think we have good reasons to do that, or should we strive to treat everyone the same?
5. According to which of the main principles discussed in this chapter do *you* most want to be treated? Why?

Chapter 3

In What Kind of Relationship Do You Want or Need to Be?

As a silly, but often revealing, icebreaker, I sometimes introduce a course section on sexual ethics with this scenario: Suppose, I say to the students, I am single. I leave the classroom and walk down the hall. A woman I consider to be very hot is walking in the other direction. She sees me and, of course, thinks that I'm hot. She says, "Do you want to have sex?" I say, "Sure, do you?" She says, "Yes," so we go find an empty room and have sex. When I ask the students if this scenario is morally problematic in any way, they typically say the following kinds of things:

- Sex is only for people who are married.
- If you want it and she wants it, go to it!
- You should at least care about someone you have sex with.
- Aren't you worried about sexually transmitted diseases and pregnancy?
- I can't imagine having sex with someone I don't really know and trust.
- Can you tell us what room you went to, so we can never go in it?

Other than the final question, which may express horror that someone of my advanced age might be having, or even thinking about, sex, these comments illustrate various versions of our next puzzle piece. In what kind of relationship does sex most appropriately happen? In this chapter, we will be exploring marriage, long-term committed relationships, relationships of mutual love, trusting friendships, and encounters based solely on consent as five possibly appropriate relationships in which to have sex. The question for you is in what kind of relationship you want or need to be when you have sex, whether for the first time or the hundredth.

In chapter 1, we focused most of our attention on what it means to truly consent to having sex. In chapter 2, we moved from pondering our own self-awareness to exploring the question of how we want to treat others. We concluded that chapter by realizing that we can harm or nurture relationships just as we can harm or nurture people. This third chapter picks up on the theme of concern for relationships by asking whether sex is more appropriate in some kinds of relationships than in others.[1]

There is a major difference in the structures of chapters 2 and 3. In chapter 2 we began by thinking about the least strict or demanding standards, such as not harming others, and moved to the stricter or more demanding, such as loving others and being willing to sacrifice for them. We will reverse directions in this chapter, beginning with the most stringent standard for having sex—marriage—and ending with the least stringent—simple consent. There is a good reason for this reversal, namely, many people's enduring default ideal that sex should be reserved for marriage.

When I tell people I am writing a book on sex, the first thing they want to know is whether I think it is morally acceptable to have sex when one is not married. My first response is that neither every instance of unmarried sex nor every instance of married sex is morally acceptable, which, of course, leads my questioner to ask whether I think *some* instances of unmarried sex are morally acceptable. When I respond that I think there are many situations in which sex between unmarried people can be not only morally justified but even enriching and life affirming, it is frequently clear that I have said something self-defining. It is as if there is a great divide between those who think sex should be reserved for marriage and those who think otherwise, and I have now declared my allegiance, to the joy or disappointment of my questioner.

I think experiences such as these reflect the grip the marriage standard continues to have on us. Maybe this is a good thing, and maybe it isn't, but it is what makes conversations about "premarital sex" occur at all. Were we all in agreement that unmarried sex could sometimes be appropriate, we would not experience what I just called the great divide between those who accept that view and those who do not. Our books, television shows, movies, and textbooks would not focus on the issue, as they often do, of whether sex is happening inside or outside of marriage, but would pay more attention to the quality of the relationships within which the sex is happening, regardless of the married state of the couple involved.

Given the prevalence and importance of the marriage standard, and given the fact that the arguments for the legitimacy of sex occurring in other contexts are often constructed with an eye to that standard, it seems reasonable to begin this chapter with the strict standard of marriage and work from there. We will begin, therefore, with a look at marriage, seeing what we think of the arguments often used to justify it as *the* appropriate place for sex. We will then look at some of the arguments in favor of other kinds of relationships as appropriate contexts for sex. My view is that many, if not all, of the kinds of relationships mentioned here, from consent to marriage, contain elements that can justify sexual intercourse. The issue is what kind of relationship you, the reader, want or need to have when you have sex, and why. What approach will help you to live your best life?

The inclusion of both "want" and "need" in this puzzle piece, by the way, is intended to capture two different states of mind. We might, for instance, *want* to be in a long-term, committed relationship the next (or first) time we have sex with someone, but we might also believe that trusted friends are legitimate sexual partners. Given that what we want (as a matter of hope or of preference for our life) and what we need (as a minimum to satisfy our moral compass) could well differ, our puzzle piece in this chapter might have a slightly more complicated shape than usual. It might include both what we would advocate as a moral minimum and what we choose for our own life.

First Context: Marriage

Before we look at several of the reasons used to support the idea that sex should only occur between two people who are married to one another, we should mention a few of the reasons that marriage itself is held in such high esteem. Here are seven reasons that are frequently offered. Do you accept any of these as good reasons to value marriage highly?

- Marriage is part of the basic order of reality that was created by God.
- Marriage is the best context within which to raise children.
- Marriage is the only truly safe space for the full development of a person.
- Less than lifelong commitment leaves a relationship incomplete.
- Marriage has significant legal advantages.
- Marriage includes a public commitment.
- Marriage serves society.

The argument that sex should be reserved for marriage rests on this foundation that considers marriage an important feature of our life together. While I am certainly not claiming here that any or all of these reasons actually justify the social structure of marriage, they are offered, separately or together, by people all around us. They constitute something of the pro-marriage climate in which we live or, to be a little more dramatic, the pro-marriage air we breathe. If some of them are successful in promoting marriage as a relational norm for us, then the notion of marriage as the appropriate context for sex has more weight than if these arguments are unsuccessful in promoting the marriage norm. Now that we have noted this foundation, here are what seem to me to be the six most frequently offered reasons for reserving sex for marriage. Which ones do you accept and which ones do you reject?

1. Sex is reserved for marriage as part of God's design.

We will explore this reason more fully in chapter 7, but it is certainly the case that many Christians are among those who believe that sex is not simply a biological function but is also a gift given by God for procreation and to promote unity within marriages.

2. Sex can be procreative.

If marriage is the correct context for raising children, as many suggest, and if, both biologically and religiously, sex has procreation as a primary purpose, then, so the argument goes, sex should be reserved for marriage. A friend who is a pastor was recently visited in his office by a young woman who said she wanted to be able to wear white authentically at her wedding someday but was currently in love and wanted to sleep with her boyfriend. She wanted to be reminded of why the church said we should not have sex before marriage. He told her that the church says this out of concern for children: We should not have sex, he said, until we are ready to do what is necessary to care for a child. Any quick response to the effect that contemporary birth control methods enable the timing of pregnancies to be planned, if they are wanted at all, can be met with reminders about the numbers of unplanned pregnancies that occur, even when birth control methods are used. If pregnancy may result from having sex, then it would seem reasonable to reserve sex for a context that is fitting for the raising of children, whatever that context may be.

3. The most intimate sexual behavior between a man and a woman should be reserved for the most intimate relationship between a man and a woman.

The argument here is grounded in a view that deems marriage the fullest and deepest expression of male-female relationship, a publicly witnessed and affirmed, emotional, intellectual, and spiritual intimacy and commitment over a lifetime that is seen nowhere else in life. It is only fitting, therefore, that the most intimate sexual connection between a man and a woman, sexual intercourse, should await the arrival in our lives of the married state. The process that moves us from being strangers to being a married couple is a process of two becoming one, not in the silly sense that we are no longer individual people when we are married, but in the sense that each step in that process brings us to greater intimacy emotionally, mentally, spiritually, and sexually. While I have heard fascinating disagreements over whether kissing is more intimate than holding hands or oral sex is more intimate than sexual intercourse, I think most of us would agree that getting to know one another sexually moves from nonsexual touching, gentle kissing, and a state of being fully dressed through more passionate kissing, sexual touching, and nakedness, to activities that might (whether or not this is our goal) produce orgasm. In this book, we are discussing vaginal intercourse as one final level of sexual intimacy. And it, so the argument goes, should be reserved for the place where the most intimate levels of the other dimensions of the person are likely to be reached, the lifelong committed married state.

4. There is only one "first time."

One person wrote this to me:

> The thing I consider most is that I only get one "first time." Given that, is this the person I want to use it on? The same for the other person: should I ask them to use their "first time" on me (or second or tenth or whatever—it would still be a consideration). The sexual relationship is the strongest connection two people can make, and it's not one that I think should be broken easily, so with that in mind, am I certain enough that this person is someone I want to make that kind of connection with?

A reason that is frequently offered for saving sex until marriage is that one's virginity, understood as innocence about sex, is a gift that can only be given once. Since the odds are that any relationship we are in before we are married is not going to be our final one, we should wait until the final and most important relationship of our lives to share that gift. It might well be said to honor a future spouse in a certain way when we reserve this gift for him or her.

5. Marriage is a protective space.

One reader said it this way:

> Marriage is a restraint or a boundary made necessary by our sinfulness. Because we are fallen and sinful creatures, all aspects of our nature, including the sexual aspects, require protective boundaries. Because of the intense physical pleasure associated with sexuality, we are prone to use it and ourselves without regard for its higher purpose of drawing us into intimate union with another. Moreover, we are prone to squander our sexuality in a desperate, impatient, faithless quest for connection with another. Marriage is a covenant of restraint that protects us against the perils to which we are prone because of sin.[2]

What does marriage protect against? It protects us from seeking sexual pleasure in situations that are likely to cause at least as much harm as good. Marriage finally gives us a place where sexual desire does not pull us in multiple directions, confusing our needs to love and be loved. In marriage, the full giftedness of sexual pleasure can be recognized, and it can be channeled into the unifying of two lives. This quotation is deeply embedded in Christian conceptions of sin, but the temptation to express our sexuality in ways that we know would be destructive of ourselves and others is a temptation most of us can recognize.

6. Sex creates a unique bond.
Finally, it is sometimes said that having sex creates a bond of some sort, a kind of union, between the two people having it, whether they recognize it or not. This bond is unique; it is not present in any human interaction other than sex, and to ignore it is to trivialize an important aspect of human relationships. Indeed, for many Christians, this bond is part of God's design for us. As one friend puts it, sex is "a window into the divine through rapturous union with another"; where else could such forces be let loose than in the set-aside space of marriage?

This is a quick look at six reasons or arguments that many people offer for saving sex for marriage. If you have an initial "gut" attraction to any of them, how would you develop it more fully? Are there any that you find especially distasteful or unhelpful? What makes you lean toward or away from the sex-only-in-marriage stance at this moment?

Second Context: Long-Term, Loving Committed Relationship

Supporters of the view that long-term, loving, committed relationships can be appropriate settings for sex, regardless of whether the two people involved believe they are heading toward marriage, build their arguments around three related concepts: commitment, mutual love, and the intention to remain together. The idea of commitment, in this sense, conveys the intention to be faithful to the partner, or faithful to whatever promises have been made to the partner. Love points to an active concern for the well-being of the other person, as well as deep feelings of affection and some kind of desire for union. If we add to these two the intention to remain together indefinitely, so the argument goes, we have a strong relationship where two people may feel safe to explore themselves and one another sexually.

A main reason offered in favor of this approach is that committed and loving, long-term relationships are what marriage is all about. Marriage is fine, if it's something you want to do, but all you are adding to the heart of your relationship is the signing of a paper and a public ceremony. If you are religious, you are also adding your sense of what God is doing in your life, but not everyone is religious, and not everyone, not even every Christian, thinks of God in the same way. Marriage is an option, but it is not significantly different, except legally, from long-term relationships; marriages even fail half of the time. What makes sex appropriate is the love, commitment, fidelity, and intention to remain together of two people, married or unmarried.

Someone who stands in the marriage camp might ask a number of questions at this point. "What about the possibility of children?" might be the first one, to which the response could well be that our long-term couple has discussed that and is ready to care for a child, should pregnancy occur. Indeed, they might say, if that happens, marriage could become an option simply because of the legal issues involved. Until then, however, they are faithfully using birth control.

Someone in the marriage camp who is also a Christian might well ask whether people in unmarried relationships having sex could be Christian. If God has given marriage to us as the appropriate place for sex to occur, then isn't it against God's way for sex to occur in any other place? The crucial issues here, for Christians, are whether God has given marriage to us and, if God has, then whether God has proclaimed that the only appropriate place for sex is within marriage. We will look at some examples of how to address these kinds of issues in chapters 7 and 11, but we can note at this point that there is great variation within Christianity on how to approach such issues. In the end, it seems to me that one could, in faith and good conscience, maintain that at least some of the alternative settings discussed in this chapter could legitimately be held by a Christian person as appropriate for sex.

Another argument for the long-term commitment approach reminds us that not everyone can marry. Gay and lesbian couples are not permitted the same legal benefits as heterosexual couples. Given this, some people declare, as a matter of justice, that they will not marry until gay and lesbian people can marry. Instead, they accept, as do many gays and lesbians, the importance of long-term (sometimes lifelong) committed relationships and see sex as appropriate to those relationships.

We should note that it is not the actual success of a relationship that makes sex appropriate here. There is no precise length of time that qualifies us as being in a "long-term" relationship. Indeed, most relationships, including fifty percent of contemporary marriages, are impermanent, but we do not know going into them which will continue and which will not. Given such uncertainty, it is the *honest intention* to make the relationship work and the loving affirmation of the other that are reasonably understood to provide good reasons for having sex by supporters of this alternate approach.

Third Context: Mutually Loving Relationship

Perhaps everyone who advocates for the long-term committed relationship as a place where sex can rightly occur includes love as part of that relationship, for why would one make a long-term romantic commitment without love? Yet love is also frequently claimed to make sex appropriate all by itself. As one person put it, "Now, I don't mean to say that I am going to marry this boy, but I do love him and trust him enough with the most special part of myself." In the words of another person, "There's definitely a part of my brain/soul that I'd have to shut off or shut up in order to have sex without love." Among the people I've spoken with who take this stance is a sense that with mutual love one feels assured that the other person cares enough to allow one to be fully vulnerable. What are the qualities of love behind this view?

First, it is mutual. Imagine the following:

> Cara and Ben are graduate students. Ben loves Cara; indeed, he lets himself think from time to time about spending his life with her. Cara enjoys their relationship, but she has yet to use, or even think, the word "love." She is getting over a previous relationship still, and work is a priority for her. She cares a lot about Ben, enjoys their friendship, and enjoys having sex with him. But she wouldn't exactly say she loves him . . . not in *that* way.

According to the mutual-love stance on the moral justification of sex, should Ben and Cara be having sex? Pretty clearly not, as the condition of mutuality is not fulfilled here. Were we standing within the trusted-friend approach (see below), we might well argue that it is appropriate for Ben and Cara to be having sex. Given our current approach, however, it seems to me we would have to consider Ben's and Cara's reasons for having sex to be insufficient. They need to have some meaningful conversation about the way they understand their relationship, sexual and otherwise. Ben needs to decide whether a trusted-friend approach is acceptable to him; Cara needs to decide whether she loves Ben.

Second, to reiterate a point we have made before, the love we are discussing here is not characterized primarily by emotions. Our understanding of love can come with so much sentimentality and triviality attached to it that we can lose sight of the fact that love has other content. This includes the creation of a safe space for both partners to be vulnerable, the partners' choosing to be vulnerable with one another, mutual trust and acceptance, encouragement for becoming the best person one can be, and a deep and active concern for the well-being of the partner. These characteristics are typically attached to feelings of affection and devotion, as well as to the drive to unite, but they are not themselves emotions. It is all of these characteristics and emotions together that make sex appropriate, according to this standard.

The mutual-love stance does not require the intention to remain together into the indefinite future. For the mutual-love approach, it is possible to say that I love you today, and I don't see that changing, but I am not going to make any long-term commitment at this point and (as long as the other person reciprocates the love, and pregnancy, STI, and consent issues are addressed) still have moral sex. What makes this possible could be a different understanding of love than the earlier two approaches (an understanding that love does not always bring with it a long-term commitment); a different understanding of sex (that it does not have to wait for emotional or spiritual intimacy to catch up with the physical intimacy of sex, for example); a different understanding of persons (that mutual love alone and not only love with commitment or love in marriage may express and enable us to be as fully human as we can be); or some combination of these. These are three of the ways one might build a foundation for the love stance.

What is the relationship between the love being discussed here and the love we discussed in chapter 2? This is an important distinction to keep in mind. Chapter 2's puzzle piece concerned how we choose to treat other people and included possibilities of not harming, fostering good, and loving. The question there concerned all people, not just family, friends, or sexual partners. On the model of the Good Samaritan, that love included the active pursuit of another person's good even at cost to the self. The love being discussed in this chapter also includes that active pursuit and cost, but it seeks union or communion with one particular other person. It is not a love that is intended for all people but a love that finds its meaning in a relationship with one other person. For many, it is this love that makes sex meaningful and appropriate. If you have it for another person, and he or she has it for you, sharing sex is a legitimate accompaniment; if you do not have it, according to this view, sex would be wrong.

Fourth Context: Trusting Friendship

Let's look at a fourth view: Love may be sufficient for morally justifying sex, but it is not necessary. If you have love or a commitment or are married, that's fine, but none of these things is needed to justify sex. When one has a friend with whom one has, over time, developed a trusting relationship, then sharing sex with that person is a morally responsible act. A friend in this sense is not a mere acquaintance and not simply a person I like but is someone I've grown to depend on to treat me well, to share parts of life with me, and to be there for me when it counts. The two of us trust each other. Under these conditions, as long as sex is consensual and safe, we may enjoy it together.

Sex, so this approach goes, is a natural part of life. Certainly, it can be manipulative, coercive, harmful, and uncaring, and that kind of sex is wrong (not because it is sex but because it is manipulative, coercive, harmful, or uncaring). But sex with someone who can be trusted with the vulnerability and nakedness that come with having sex, someone with whom we can laugh and have fun and share ideas and enjoy pleasure, is morally acceptable and adds another layer to the friendship. "I don't know whether I love him," one person said to me recently, "but the sex is wonderful, and he is a great friend."

We quoted above a possible rejoinder to this:

> The sexual relationship is the strongest connection two people can make, and it's not one that I think should be broken easily, so with that in mind, am I certain enough that this person is someone I want to make that kind of connection with?

If we accept the trusted-friendship approach, how might we respond to this? We might argue that the sexual connection is *not*, in and of itself, the strongest connection two people can make, but that what makes it strong is the context. If it happens between friends, it creates less of a connection than it does if it happens between two people who love each other and are committed to each other, but that's okay. An alternative way to say this might be that the most important thing to consider in deciding among these approaches is the meaning we want to give to sex, because it has no intrinsic meaning.

To that attempt to defend the trusted-friendship stance, a critic might respond as another person did above: "There's definitely a part of my brain/ soul that I'd have to shut off or shut up in order to have sex without love." For many people, the very experience of sex comes with meaning attached to it. Whether or not one is a Christian, the vulnerability of sex may be experienced as a soul-touching event. Of course, we don't know this until we become to some extent sexually active, and this is one reason some resist this friendship stance. If, they say, we need to have sex to know the meaning of sex, if it isn't just a theoretical matter, then perhaps we should wait until we are sure we are not going to find out that the meaning of sex is something our current context cannot handle. A possible response, of course, is that good friends touch our souls in many ways, and sex is another appropriate way for us to share with one another.

You can see, I hope, how this conversation might proceed between someone who accepts the trusted-friend approach and someone who does not. Where do you stand? We have one more stance to go, but, at least at this point, where do you think sex gets whatever meaning it has?

Fifth Context: Consensual Encounter

Remember the icebreaker I mentioned at the beginning of this chapter? I'm walking down the hall, meet a woman who wants to have sex with me, and we have sex. This is the final shape of this puzzle piece that I will discuss here. It says that all you need to justify having sex is two consenting people. Of course, STIs and pregnancy must be addressed, but once those issues are out of the way, this view says that sex between strangers who meet in the hallway or at a party or on the beach is just fine.

The first thing we need to say here is that consent on the part of both parties provides the minimal possible justification for having sex. We ruled out nonconsensual sex in the first chapter, so even if we have some work to do to discern exactly what consent is, we can at least say that right sex requires consent.

Those who accept this view do so for a number of different reasons. For some, it is simply the case that within limits of consent, safety, and lack of harm, sex is no more "special" than any number of other human acts of closeness. A married twenty-something wrote, "Sex is quite a bit of fun, but in general I don't experience it as some deeply spiritual act that brings us any closer than, say, Saturday morning waffles or going hiking. Sometimes it is, but sometimes it's just basic recreation." For a second group, sex is simply a natural expression of the pleasure pursuit between two people, designed by biological forces, and the more of it they can get the better. Moments of mutual pleasure (a gift from God, some who are Christian might offer) with another person are great things. God, after all, respects so much that we do in the name of freedom; why not sex for pleasure? A third group might focus on the nature of consent itself, arguing that it is the backbone of all manner of important connections in society, and ask whether it makes any sense to change that for something as simple and natural as sex. Consensual sex respects our freedom as human beings, the goodness of pleasure, and the human need to touch and be touched; how, we might ask, could it be wrong? What do you think?

Concluding Thoughts

There are two points we should be sure do not get lost in these complex discussions. The first is that, typically, those who advocate the marriage context argue that all of the other contexts are part of marriage. Indeed, those who advocate any of the contexts argue that the less stringent standards are included in theirs. This is important, among other reasons, because it reminds us that sex without consent is wrong, no matter which context one advocates. Nonconsensual intercourse in marriage is still rape. The notion is also important because it raises the questions of whether broken trust in a long-term committed relationship or the absence of love, in the sense here defined, in a marriage makes sex in those contexts inappropriate. Answers will vary, but the debate has significant bearing on the shape of our relationships.

Second, I believe we would be wrong, as I have said, to see only one or two of these stances as possible for Christians to hold. Although harm to self and others (and sin, within the Christian perspective) can infect relationships in any of the contexts, each one of them expresses and even celebrates some gift of God. The mutual-consent approach celebrates one of God's greatest gifts to humanity, the gift of freedom. Used consensually and protectively, it gives thanks also for the pleasure of sexual connection with another person. Trusted friendships show God's gift of human interdependence, of human community, and of being accepted as we are. Love is, according to many, the very essence of God, and human expressions of it remind us of God's love for us and faithfulness to us. The intention to remain together through life's ups and downs reinforces our awareness of God's faithfulness and gives thanks for the possibility of lifelong companionship. And marriage, whether or not considered a sacrament, underscores the presence of God with us and the union that is our final destiny with God. Each of these contexts might be held by a Christian to justify sex, even if only one reflects the dominant view of the biblical and church traditions through history. Whether this dominant view is a correct view is a question with which it is well worth wrestling.

In chapter 1, you put significant thought into the kinds of information and level of awareness of relevant factors that you need in order to have sex with someone. In chapter 2, you paid close attention to the issue of how you want to be treating people in life, both generally and in your sexual encounters or relationships. I hope you have made good progress in sorting out the shape those two puzzle pieces will take in your final solution to the puzzle of whether to have sex. In this chapter, five options (and any other intermediate ones you might have been inspired to create along the way) have been presented to you as possible shapes for your third puzzle piece. Have you chosen one? Do you think mutual consent provides you with a sufficient reason to have sex with someone? How about trust and friendship? Love? Do you think it is important to share sex only in long-term committed relationships, which include both love and trust? Are you convinced that marriage is the only right place in which to have sex? Whichever one you choose, how would you support your view in a conversation with representatives from the other approaches? These decisions are now in your hands, as you complete this third piece of the puzzle.

Questions for Reflection and Discussion

1. For better or for worse, none of us can know what today's relationship will look like tomorrow. Does that fact shape your thinking about when sex is or is not appropriate?
2. I have made some rather bold claims in this chapter about what Christians can legitimately believe. If you are a Christian, on what grounds would you agree with me or disagree with me?
3. If you are in a relationship of one of the kinds described here and are having sex, is it working for you? Have you found a context within which you know it is right to have sex? How do you know? What seems right or wrong about your sexual life right now?
4. If you have had sex with more than one person, has this been within more than one of the contexts described here? If so, what have you learned that you could pass on to others?

Chapter 4

If You Do Not Wish to Become Pregnant, How Will You Prevent It?

*E*ach time I climb behind the wheel of my car, I say a short prayer that I won't harm anyone or be harmed while driving. I don't actually think God will be intervening to keep me, among all the people on the road at the time, from having an accident, though the practice may be left over from when I did think such things. Now, my prayer is more a way of reminding myself to be careful, to pay attention while driving, to drive defensively instead of offensively. It's my acknowledgment that, statistically speaking, there is a certain degree of risk attached to what I am about to do but that the value I attach to the freedoms represented by my mobility and to the purposes of this particular trip outweighs the value I attach to the risk of having an accident.

The logic of unplanned pregnancy is a bit like the logic of this example. Whether or not an unplanned and unwanted pregnancy is a "harm," it can be a nightmare. Even a pregnancy "scare" can cause enormous emotional and relational upheaval, as these words from Elizabeth suggest:

> I had just graduated from high school and was in the middle of living it up as hard as I could before I went to college. Midway through the summer I realized I was two weeks late for my period. At first I didn't know what to do. Pretend like it wasn't real, or talk about it? I chose to discuss it with my two best girl friends. We decided I should take a pregnancy test. Do I tell the boy? HELL NO. Why? If I'm pregnant, I will get rid of it, plain and simple. No doubt about it. I won't ever tell him OR my parents OR ANY-ONE. It will be like it never happened. I think I knew that I would rather abort in silence and live with the guilt for the rest of my life than face my parents. I was NOT going to be that girl: [the] irresponsible, loose girl who threw her life away. Poor, sad thing. Pathetic. Unintelligent. Unmarried. "Her poor parents and younger sister," they would say. "How did she go wrong?" they would ask. I could see it all.

Elizabeth was grateful when she found out she was not pregnant. When we have sex as unmarried people, especially as unmarried and not particularly attached people, we typically hope we do not become pregnant. Statistically, of course, some of us will have our hopes left unfulfilled, and we will need to wrestle with what to do next. However, assuming we are making our choice with a clear mind and heart, we choose to have sex because, as with driving, we judge that the benefits outweigh the risks. This chapter focuses on the risk of unwanted pregnancy and asks how we will attempt to minimize the risk of becoming pregnant. The next chapter continues the exploration of unwanted pregnancy, asking what we will do if our attempt fails. These are our fourth and fifth puzzle pieces. Exploring your answers will enable you, by working backward, to reflect on whether you are going to have sex.

Here are a couple of things to keep in mind as we work through this chapter and the next. First, I remember a married couple excitedly announcing their pregnancy to a roomful of friends. Later that evening, they whispered to me, "We need to be more careful; we didn't expect this!" Their delight, however, was palpable. Even if unwanted pregnancies can be like nightmares, wanted pregnancies, even if unplanned, can be dreams come true for many people. We are all heirs to powerful hopes, desires, and traditions that see children as blessings; when these come together, they can make pregnancies joyous events. Even though we will be focusing on pregnancies that occur in contexts that make them unwanted, we want to keep in mind that this is not the only context for pregnancy.

Second, these chapters are intended for both men and women. My impression is that the law is catching up with the notion that two people are responsible for pregnancies (so, for instance, men are financially responsible for their children, whether or not they are currently in a relationship with the mother), and some people's attitudes are catching up, but the moral reality of mutual responsibility has always existed. We will recognize this here by speaking to men as much as women in everything we say. For instance, "Unless you want to become pregnant" means "Unless you (male or female) want to become pregnant." It is important to do what we can to heighten recognition of mutual responsibility for and decision making about birth control, pregnancy, and sex.

At the same time as we work to bolster the sense and fact of male-female mutual responsibility, we need to recognize that a disproportionate share of responsibility for preventing pregnancy, caring for pregnancy, and caring for children has always fallen to women. Women typically carry more of the anxiety attached to the possibility of pregnancy, and they know the reality of pregnancy with an immediacy men cannot. Whatever their moral and legal responsibility, men also have the choice to walk away from dealing with an unwanted pregnancy in a way women cannot. While we will assume a sense and reality of co-responsibility here because of its moral rightness, it's crucial to recognize the degree of idealism behind that assumption.

We have, then, our fourth puzzle piece: As you ponder whether to have sex, how will you deal with the possibility of an unwanted pregnancy? How will you take responsibility for minimizing the risk of such a pregnancy? Should pregnancy occur, would you want to raise the child, put the child up for adoption, or have an abortion? How do your answers to these questions contribute to your decision about having sex? We will begin with a look at some issues about birth control.

Birth Control

Here's a story from a forty-something named Robert:

> I dated a girl named Nina for about five years back in my mid-twenties. We had sex before we dated; as a matter of fact, the first time we had sex, we had only seen each other for a few moments total, over the course of a few weeks. One of her housemates was dating one of my housemates, and Nina and her housemate were over visiting one night. She heard some of her favorite music coming from my room and wandered in to say hi. Someone started talking about backrubs, and soon I was giving her one. I remember thinking, just before we had sex, that I didn't really know her, that I had no idea whether she was on birth control or whether she slept around or had a sexually transmitted infection or anything at all. But, I really wanted to have sex with her, so I did. Sometime afterward, I was able to calm down enough to say something about birth control. She said she usually used a diaphragm, but didn't have it with her. Her period had just ended, though, she said, so she wasn't going to worry about it. I worried.

There is some evidence that young men, at least, make different decisions when sexually aroused than they would make when not aroused.[1] Pretty clearly, Robert's brain was trying to get him to ponder other possibilities than having risky sex. But the drive was too strong for him and probably for Nina as well. This is one of those edge-of-the-pool instances: If you don't know how to swim, so the saying goes, don't race around the edge of the pool. If you aren't ready to have sex, don't get so close to having it that you can't stop.

Obviously, one of the decisions that faced Robert and Nina, even though they failed to address it, was what kind of birth control to use. While I am not making medical recommendations here, and the choice of what birth control method you decide to use or not to use is a decision best made on the basis of good medical advice, the following six questions might contribute meaningfully to your thinking on this issue.

1. Do you have any religious convictions that shape your views on birth control?

Most Christian denominations and groups believe that sex between unmarried people is wrong, so their discussions of birth control tend to be directed toward married couples. Many of these discussions convert easily to our context, however, so let's just note two and see whether they shape your thinking in any way.

The Learning Channel's popular series *19 Kids and Counting* follows the lives of Michelle and Jim Bob Duggar and their family, whose version of Christianity precludes the use of birth control. As they explain on their Web site, Michelle's second pregnancy happened when she was on the pill, and she miscarried between her second and third month.

> When the doctor told us the miscarriage probably happened because she had conceived while still on the pill, we were devastated. To us, it meant that something we had chosen to do—use the pill—had caused the end of the pregnancy. As conservative Christians, we believe that every life is sacred, even the life of the unborn. Due to our lack of knowledge, we destroyed the precious life of our unborn child. We prayed and studied the Bible and found a host of references that told us God considered children a gift, a blessing, and a reward. Yet we had considered having another child an inconvenience during that busy time in our lives, and we had taken steps to prevent it from happening. We weren't sure if Michelle could have any more children after the miscarriage, but we were sure we were going to stop using the pill. In fact we agreed we would stop using any form of birth control and let God decide how many children we would have.[2]

Whether or not you accept this view, it presents an opportunity to think carefully about God's involvement in pregnancy. For Christians, the idea that God is intimately involved in the world is a given, but exactly *how* God is involved may vary almost from Christian to Christian. Since we don't have a precise view given to us here, what are the possible meanings of "let God decide how many children we would have"? It could be a metaphor that means something like the following: Whether pregnancy does or does not happen should be seen as one of the universe's great mysteries, and we will simply treat however many pregnancies and children we have as gifts from

God. It could mean something very literal: God makes decisions about how many children people will have and ensures that those pregnancies and births will occur, so we should simply accept however many children we do or do not have as God's intention for us. Either way, the result is not to interfere with conception in any way, though the question of whether we can, even if we so desire, block God's decisions arises only with the second, literal sense.

Roman Catholicism also sees artificial birth control as morally and spiritually indefensible. Pope Paul VI, in the well-known 1968 encyclical *Humanae Vitae*, wrote, "Similarly [to abortion and sterilization] excluded is any action which either before, at the moment of, or after sexual intercourse, is specifically intended to prevent procreation—whether as an end or as a means."[3] Every act of sexual intercourse must, in the official Catholic view, be open to new life being formed. While forms of natural family planning, such as attempting to restrict sex to those times in a woman's cycle when conception is least likely to occur, are permissible, these are not "artificial" methods of placing a barrier in nature's (God's) way; they cooperate with nature and do not attempt to control it. Further, in a view that is echoed in many circles, Christian and otherwise, Catholicism argues that the availability of birth control contributes to our climate of widespread illicit sex. To see their point, ask yourself this question: Would you have sex if no birth control were available? If your answer is "Probably not," then you understand the force of this part of the Catholic argument.

Perhaps the most important question for you to ponder at this point is whether you think God is involved in conception, pregnancy, or having children in a way that would prevent you from using one or more kinds of birth control. Is procreation a natural process without any spiritual dimensions that might shape whether or not we try to prevent conception? Or, to name one alternative, does God have plans for when and how many children each of us has, and are we tampering with God's plans when we prevent or postpone conception? Next, apply your views on this question to our larger issue: Do you have any religious reflections on birth control that would shape your views on having sex at a time when you are not open to pregnancy?

2. How do the methods work?

We are regularly encouraged to be informed about the medicines we take and the medical technologies we use, to try to understand how these things work so that we are partners in our own care and not mere objects of medical attention. Understanding what happens when we become pregnant and how various birth control methods prevent that from happening is part of this cooperation in self-care. As noted, you will want to rely on medical sources and medical professionals for a real understanding of these issues, but we can at least get started in the right direction.

To begin, here's a quick primer on pregnancy. Monthly, a woman's ovaries release one of her finite number of eggs. It moves into the nearest fallopian tube, which connects the ovary to the uterus. Sperm from the man travels up through the vagina, through the cervix, which is the opening to the uterus, and into the fallopian tube, where it fertilizes the egg it meets there. In a normal pregnancy, the fertilized egg travels down to the uterus, where it attaches to the uterine wall in a process known as implantation. These few, simplified facts give us what we need to know to understand how birth control methods work.

Most of you have heard it said over and over again that the only fully reliable form of birth control is abstinence. Although abstinence programs in general have proven themselves to be fairly unsuccessful in preventing sex and unwanted pregnancy,[4] it is always worth remembering that there is nothing that requires you to have sex. One reasonable response to this book's question of whether you want to have sex now is "No," and that is not only a logical answer from the point of view of preventing pregnancy but also an answer that may reflect your best understanding of yourself and how you want to be living your life. If you think you might be answering "Yes" to the book's question, however, pondering other forms of birth control becomes more relevant to you.

. Hormonal contraceptives (including pills, rings, patches, and shots like Depo-Provera) attempt to stop the woman's ovaries from releasing an egg, thereby preventing fertilization. The progesterone hormone in these contraceptives also thickens the mucus covering the cervix, making it more difficult for sperm to reach any egg that might be released. In case fertilization does occur, which can occasionally happen with these contraceptives, progesterone may, at least theoretically, make implantation of a fertilized egg in the uterus less likely. It is this last, however unusual, possibility that leads some people to think of hormonal contraceptives as abortion-causing, on the assumption that they might lead to the expulsion of a fertilized egg.

Intrauterine devices (IUDs), considered safer these days than the versions used several decades ago, are T-shaped devices placed into the uterus. Like hormonal contraceptives, they contain artificial progesterone (progestin), which makes cervical mucus thicker than usual and prevents fertilization by making it harder for sperm to make it to the uterus. Should the rare fertilization occur, IUDs might also be able to prevent implantation. In addition, the copper out of which some IUDs are made is lethal to sperm.

Barrier methods of birth control simply try to keep the sperm and the egg apart. Male condoms aim to collect the sperm in the condom before it reaches any available egg (and may also, of course, give some protection against STIs). Female condoms, diaphragms, contraceptive sponges, and other barriers that a woman might use, often combined with a spermicide, aim to block sperm from entering the uterus by covering the cervical opening and killing approaching sperm. Should sperm get beyond the barrier and the spermicide, pregnancy is certainly possible, and there is no backup plan here for disenabling implantation.

Does this brief reflection on birth control methods give you any initial thoughts on what would be right for you? Some people are bothered by even the theoretical possibility that some methods may cause a fertilized egg not to be implanted in the uterus; does this bother you? If you were to choose a method for yourself at this moment, what would it be, and why? Does any piece of this discussion shape your thinking about having sex?

3. What level of effectiveness are you seeking?

Obviously, if your intention is to prevent pregnancy, one of the most important things you will want to know is whether a particular method is effective in achieving this end. In other words, how well does it work? There is significant variation among the methods on this point, depending in part on how well the method is used, and most sources will report both perfect usage and typical usage. In general, Depo-Provera, the pill, and the IUD are the most effective methods, running anywhere from 97 percent to over 99 percent effective, depending on the method and the usage. Barrier methods are much less reliable, when used alone, with the male condom falling well below 90 percent in actual usage.

How does the slight possibility of becoming pregnant with virtually any form of birth control you use shape your decision about the conditions under which you will have sex? The use of more than one method (e.g., Depo-Provera and male condoms) increases your chances of avoiding pregnancy, of course, but abstinence from sex is the only alternative that will actually promise that you can avoid it. Yet, for many of us, the pleasures and emotional connections that can come with sex make the risk of pregnancy worth it. For others of us, of course, the possibility of facing an unplanned pregnancy means we will not be having sex until and unless we are ready for children. Perhaps the most important thing to remember is that we each must be comfortable with whatever risk we decide to take; no one else gets to make this choice for us.

The next three issues can be stated more briefly than the previous three. They remain important, however, so we don't want to ignore them.

4. What health concerns do you have?

Part of learning how given birth control methods work is coming to understand what they do when they are inside or in contact with your body. Most methods will have some side effects, and these may be positive or negative or both. The pill, for example, in one or more of its forms, may be prescribed for the alleviation of severe menstrual cramps, a positive effect, but it can also have negative side effects such as blood clots. If these issues can be explored in conjunction with your partner, all the better.

5. What about safer sex?

As we discussed in an earlier chapter, one prominent health concern faced by many who choose to have sex these days is sexually transmitted infections. The method of birth control that provides the most meaningful help in this arena is the male condom. Indeed, if you are not absolutely sure (or as close to that as is humanly possible) that your partner has no STI, pretty much everyone who ponders these things agrees that using a condom is the way to go. Not everyone likes them, of course: Some do not like the emotional effects of having a barrier between themselves and their partner; some men do not like the lessened sensitivity attached to some condoms; and stopping to put one on can lessen the excitement of the moment. On the other hand, putting on a condom is easily made a part of foreplay, and this is another situation where we have to think carefully about what risks we are willing to take. Perhaps more importantly, we might consider *why* we are willing to take any at all, with respect to this particular issue. What do you think? Are there conditions under which you would feel fine about *not* using a condom when having sex with someone? If not, are there ways you can guarantee that you won't become so aroused at some point that you act against what you think best?

6. How will you share the costs for the form of birth control you use?

There are a number of different kinds of costs associated with obtaining and using birth control. These may include costs of time, perhaps for thinking about which method to use or for a trip to the pharmacy; costs in money, for such things as gas in your car or medical appointments or the birth control itself; the cost of the embarrassment some may experience at buying condoms; or the cost of the discomfort some may feel at a gynecological appointment. To suggest that you might look for ways to share costs with your partner is not to suggest that everything in life that involves two people should, or even could, always be split evenly; it is simply to say that there are costs attached to the obtaining of birth control methods, and who is to carry these and why are reasonable issues to address.

Exploring the options for birth control may lead you in one or another direction as you ponder whether you want to have sex. Assuming you decide to have sex and do not wish to become pregnant, you will want to use one or another birth control method. Despite your best intentions, of course, you still might become pregnant. At that point, three broad options would face you: raising or co-raising the child, putting the child up for adoption, or having an abortion. We will explore each of these in our next chapter.

Questions for Reflection and Discussion

1. Are you currently having sex? What form(s) of birth control are you using? Why did you choose those forms? If you are not currently having sex, but are thinking about it, what form(s) are you considering using, and why?
2. Have you ever had a pregnancy scare? How did you feel? What was the outcome? Elizabeth said that she stopped having sex for a period of time after her scare. How about you? What had to happen before you started having sex again?
3. What is your response to the idea of talking with your partner about sharing the costs associated with birth control?

Chapter 5

What If You Become Pregnant?

At the beginning of the previous chapter, you read the story of Elizabeth's pregnancy scare. Elizabeth had another such scare a number of years later, and this is what she wrote about that one:

> This scare was quite different because I did, in fact, have some respectable aspects to my situation: I was engaged to be married, and it would be my future husband's baby in my belly, not my eighteen-year-old, juvenile, pot-smoking fling's baby. I had come a long way toward being a more responsible self. I was in love, engaged, supported; I was doing great. And then this little snag appeared. I was, again, two weeks late on my period. This time though, my (now) husband knew about every moment, almost every emotion. We had the same questions; we had (almost) the same fears: I am not ready to be a parent. Our lives together have just started. We didn't make it to the wedding. What will people think of us? At least we are engaged. What will our families think? We appear irresponsible and reckless. How could we have let this happen? What will we do for money? When will we have the wedding? Abortion did cross my mind, only because it was a solution to the problem that would eliminate all the hard and tough questions. I knew I couldn't do it though. I would feel devastated for the rest of my life for aborting a potential first child with my husband, the man I am madly in love with. I did want to have kids with him, but just not yet. Right before the time when it would be okay—as in right before the wedding. I still had fear and shame in my heart when I thought about facing my parents, but I had the knowledge that I was with the man I was going to marry to settle those fears.

Once again, Elizabeth's fears were unfounded, and she learned in another week or so that she was not pregnant. I'm introducing this chapter, which focuses on your fifth puzzle piece, with her story not because it is a story about having and raising a child, which it isn't, but because it illustrates the

51

fact that the context of our lives at the moment of decision is one of the things that shape what we do. That's not a surprise, certainly, but it points to one place we can look to create some helpful questions for our own discernment process, even though it is not always easy to discern what elements of someone's context will make a difference in his or her momentous choices. Sometimes, we seem to act against what appears, on the surface, to be possible for us. Kathleen's story, which is an example of this, begins our section on choosing to raise a child.

Choosing to Raise a Child

> I thought we would be together forever when we had sex. My period had been so messed up that I barely noticed when I missed it for two months. The pregnancy test was positive. I couldn't believe it. How could I take care of a baby when I could barely take care of myself? Oh, God. I was ashamed and scared of what people would say. They were going to see me. I couldn't hide. I had no boyfriend, no money, no insurance. My only thought was, I can't do this.

Kathleen's road was a difficult one, filled with financial challenges, problems with health and health care, difficulty finding appropriate and affordable housing, difficulty finding good child care, struggles with unreliable transportation to work, and custody conflicts. But, in the end, Kathleen changed her entire life to provide for her child, and she is successfully and lovingly raising him. How did she do it? Three things probably made the difference, and even some close observers would have missed every one of them and predicted she would not have the child. First, Kathleen's mother provided Kathleen and the new grandson with sustained emotional support, even though from the other side of the country. Second, extended family members jumped in and provided some financial assistance. Third, Kathleen had an inner strength and determination that came from never expecting life to be easy. The context of her life made all the difference, even though that context was not immediately obvious to anyone, including Kathleen.

Let's add to these two brief examples a more extended one. See if you can discern in the several examples any questions that might shed light on your decision about having sex. Tami wrote this:

> Mark and I were "friends with benefits" before we really started dating. I was on the pill, though we were both aware that I didn't always take it as directed. Besides, due to a childhood illness, Mark was told by his doctors

that it was unlikely he would be able to father children. A year or so after we started having sex, and two days after we broke up, I discovered I was pregnant. Over the next few hours, I was embarrassed, scared, angry with myself, and hysterical. I felt stupid and alone. When I told Mark, he took it better than I had, and we talked about getting back together. In trying to decide what to do, I thought of everything: How would I finish school? My dad had always said he would disown me if I got pregnant; how would I tell my parents? Where would I live? Mark and I had just broken up out of frustration and stress; did we really love each other enough to do this? Mark wanted me to have an abortion, because he said he couldn't afford to raise a family now. I thought about it and talked with a friend about it and researched it, but decided I couldn't have an abortion. I wasn't sure what I believed about God, and I didn't know if I thought abortion was murder, but I did know that if I had an abortion, I would always wonder if I had done the right thing. I remember walking around campus after that realization, with my hand pressed against my abdomen, crying and saying, "It's my job to keep you safe." I talked with Mark again, and he supported my feelings. We talked about adoption, but I knew that there would be no way I could let go of a baby I had carried for nine months and that, again, I would always feel guilty about that decision. We decided to raise the child, somehow. Telling our parents was very rough; in the end, they accepted the direction we chose. Our friends were incredibly supportive. We left school, Mark found a job, and we moved closer to our families. Life could be a lot easier than it is, but somehow I know I am supposed to be a mother; Mark and I are pleased with where life has taken us to this point, and we are expecting our second child soon.

What questions have these scenarios suggested that might get you thinking about your willingness to take the risk of becoming pregnant? Let's take a quick look at five:

1. What is the nature of your relationship with your sexual partner?
2. What does your broader support system look like?
3. What do you know about yourself?
4. Are you ready for a life to be dependent on you?
5. What changes are you ready to make?

I am well aware, by the way, that these kinds of questions are often asked in a tone intended almost to intimidate people into not having sex. I trust you understand, by now, that I am in no way trying to do that. Indeed, I have already noted that I think sex between unmarried people can sometimes be morally appropriate. One of the things that can make it so, however, is being ready to accept its possible consequences. This is a matter for both logical and moral reflection, but there is nothing in it that should be read as chastising or intimidating. Even if the risk is very low, when I drive, I accept the possibility that I will harm someone or be harmed. When I lift weights, I accept the possibility that I will end up with an injury. The pleasures, hopes, and needs attached to driving or working out make the risk worth it, but I should be aware of the possibilities in order to make a clear decision for myself and others. The same is true of having sex. The benefits may be worth the risks, but we can't know that until we ponder both the benefits and the risks. These questions are intended to help us do just that.

1. What is the nature of your relationship with your sexual partner?

After expecting her partner to be around forever, Kathleen discovered that she was going to be alone in facing her pregnancy and raising her child. In her pregnancy scares, Elizabeth didn't want her "fling" to know about her possible pregnancy in the first case, but she shared everything with her fiancé the second time. Tami had just broken up with her boyfriend when she found out she was pregnant, but she and Mark got back together and raised the baby together. Despite our best plans and hopes, our relationships don't always take the shape we think they will, which makes it difficult, obviously, to anticipate what a relationship with a sexual partner might look like if pregnancy occurs. Yet we can certainly, in a quiet moment alone, reflect on whether we are ready to parent alone (if the other person opts out) or coparent a child. Would he be a good father? Would she be a good mother? Of course, the future is impossible to know, but even if the odds are one in a thousand of pregnancy occurring, pondering what it would be like to raise a child with your sexual partner, who may or may not demand a place at the table, might help in thinking about whether you want to have sex with her or him.

2. What does your broader support system look like?

In Elizabeth's case, a friend gave her good emotional support during her first pregnancy scare, and her fiancé stood by her in the second. Kathleen ultimately found support of various kinds from family members. Friends of both Tami and Mark made a huge difference in Tami's case. Do you have family or friends you would trust to be supportive during pregnancy and beyond? How does your answer shape how you are thinking about sex?

3. What do you know about yourself?

It is often truly said that we do not know what we are capable of until we are really tested. At the same time, what do a little introspection and your "gut" tell you about yourself? Both Kathleen and Tami had serious reservations about their ability to raise their children. Kathleen probably would not have said, had we asked her, that she is a strong and determined woman. Although Tami did not at first realize it before the pregnancy, she later said, "I am supposed to be a mom and I love it." Both of them gave up going out drinking with friends when they learned they were pregnant, though both of them enjoyed those social times very much; this was simply a matter of knowing what they had to do and doing it. Are you good at knowing what you have to do and doing it? Do you have hidden strengths that you believe would rise up and serve you well if you found yourself having to raise a child?

4. Are you ready for a life to be dependent on you?
"How can I take care of a baby when I can't even take care of myself?" asked Kathleen, and we can imagine that she would have answered, "No" to this fourth question. Ready or not, however, she made it work, as did Tami and Mark, and as have so many other single people and couples through the centuries. It is frequently noted that no one is actually ready to have children; we learn as we go what it *really* means to put someone else first in life. So maybe the question here is not so much about readiness but more about desire: *Do you want to be responsible for another life at this moment in your own life*? If not, does that realization in any way influence your decision to have sex?

5. What changes are you ready to make?
I noted that both Kathleen and Tami stopped going out drinking with friends. Kathleen looked for a better job and improved living conditions. Tami left school. I imagine you could easily list many changes that would enter your life if you were pregnant and had decided to raise the child. You might need a decent job right away, if you don't have one. Your friendships might change, as the activities of caring for the pregnancy could easily decrease your contact with some of your friends. As a woman, your image of your body and self might well change. As a man, you would be seen very differently as an expectant father than as a guy who sleeps with his girlfriend. Making a quick list of likely changes could help a bit with gaining clarity on the overall issue of whether to have sex. What changes do you think you would have to make, and would they be easy or hard for you or the person you want to become?

These are the kinds of questions that might help you ponder whether you are ready to place yourself in the position of having sex. Perhaps you can look at the scenarios in this chapter, ponder these questions, add some questions of your own, and decide that yes, you believe that if you became pregnant and could not see abortion or adoption as viable possibilities, you would have the support and determination to raise a child, alone or with the person with whom you are having sex. Perhaps you look at all of these things and decide that you are not ready. In that case, the issue is whether you see the benefits of having sex as significant enough to risk placing yourself in a situation for which you are not ready. What do you think?

Choosing Adoption

Another option available to us if we become pregnant is giving birth and placing the child up for adoption. There are hundreds of thousands of couples and many single people waiting to adopt and love a child they cannot have or have chosen not to have on their own. Placing a child up for adoption requires facing some of the challenges we have already seen—the visibility of pregnancy and, therefore, having to tell people about it; emotional and financial support during pregnancy; and probably some changes in behavior on your part. Let's just look briefly at a story that brings out two additional dimensions of the adoptive process: grief and gift giving.

Back in my graduate school days, I spent a couple of years working on assembly lines. In one job, there was a young woman whom I'll call Jen on a line right next to me. She had become pregnant at sixteen and had given her child up for adoption. She often wanted to talk about him, especially on important occasions such as his birthday, and always did so with the sound of loss in her voice. She said she often tried to pick him out in crowds, even though the adoption was "closed," so she had no idea what he now looked like. One day, she said, more or less out of the blue, "I think I saw him at the fair yesterday," or at least a boy who was the right age and had her skin tone with her ex-boyfriend's hair. She was still experiencing a good bit of grief four or five years after the adoption. She described it as something like losing her uncle to death, except that her son wasn't, as far as she knew, dead. It seemed her grief was always somewhat incomplete, because she couldn't get to the place of saying that he was gone as she could when her uncle died. She was always looking and wondering, never quite fully letting go. It was sometimes a hard place to live.

In addition to the kind of grief Jen felt, we should not pass over the grief that some adopted children feel. Friends of mine who are adopted have sometimes expressed feeling a kind of grief of their own, as they puzzled over why they had been placed with other families. Were they not wanted? Was it somehow their fault? At least two of them have found and reached out to their birth mothers. In one case, this began a long and good mother-daughter friendship; the other friend had a door slammed in her face. For whatever reason, one mother could handle bringing her child back into her life, and one could not. In the latter case, my friend found other family members who were delighted and welcoming. Both of these friends, by the way, were very happy with their adoptive parents and were leading good lives, but there was a hole somewhere, and they wanted to find out more about the chapters of their own stories that were mysterious to them.

Even as my coworker grieved the loss of her son, she seemed to feel some reassurance and even happiness in the hope that the child was receiving much better care than she could have provided. The father had been no one she wanted to remain in a relationship with, much less marry, and she had known that she was emotionally "just a kid" herself, with a family that had no interest in raising the child. For her son's own good, she placed him through an agency with an unknown set of parents, and she believed he was "better off" than he would have been with her.

In the midst of her very mixed feelings, Jen carried with her a sense, usually muted, that she had given a great *gift*. Part of this came from her conviction that she had acted in the best interests of her child, but part of it was her recognition that there was a couple out there in the world somewhere who had received from her something—someone—they were longing for. She had, in recognition of her own circumstances in life and with love for her child, given him up, and she knew that, for this unknown couple, her sacrifice was a significant gift. That pleased her.

Of course, so-called "closed" adoptions, such as the one with which Jen was involved, are not the only possibility. In open adoptions, significant amounts of identifying information may be shared between the birth parents and the adopting parents, and there may even be relationships of some kinds established among all the parties. Although this approach is not for everyone, it does have the potential to alter some of the sense of grief and loss that the birth parents may feel. As you can imagine, there can be complicated legal issues here, and obtaining legal advice is necessary before deciding on one type of adoption or another.

How do you think you should weigh these things as you think about the possibility of becoming pregnant and trying to decide what to do? We might say that we never want to cause anyone grief, including ourselves, so placing a child up for adoption would just not be a reasonable choice for us. Or we might say that grief can be hard, but the benefits of adoption (for the person who does not feel able to care for the child, and especially for the child and for those longing to adopt) far outweigh even a lifetime of grief. How do you weigh the good of a gift made in sacrificial love and with the intention of meeting the best interests of a child against the emotional holes that might be left in people's lives by this process? How do these things shape your thinking about becoming pregnant and. following the logical trail backward, about having sex?

Choosing Abortion

Let's take stock of where we are. You are deciding, perhaps a bit theoretically and perhaps quite practically, whether to have sex. I have proposed that we understand this and other significant moral problems as puzzles to be solved. In this chapter and the previous one, we are looking at your fourth and fifth puzzle pieces, the fourth and fifth sets of issues that, as you make choices in response to them, will fit together with the pieces from the other chapters of the book to provide you with at least a tentative answer to your moral question. These issues are about unplanned and unwanted pregnancies, and their logic is simple. Sex will, in some circumstances, lead to pregnancy. When we are pregnant, we have three major choices: raise the child, place the child for adoption, or have an abortion. If we are not ready for or do not want to face any of those, then we will not have sex or we will use some method of birth control that is 100 percent effective and safe. Since there are no such methods, we must weigh the benefits of having sex, on the one hand, against the possibilities of pregnancy for the method we choose and our assessment of our ability to face pregnancy, should it occur, on the other. So far in this chapter, we have looked at the experience of pregnancy "scares," some issues related to birth control, and the options of having children and choosing adoption. We are now going to look at the final issues of the chapter, those related to abortion.

In my experience, the number of people who want to become involved in a serious discussion about abortion these days is rather small. Most "discussions" soon become heated, quieting those voices that are not interested in fighting. In other discussions, it becomes clear that the parties' starting places are so different that no progress is likely to be made. And most of the time, as one of my graduate school professors used to say, the arguments should just be numbered, because we have heard them all before and could save ourselves a lot of time by just saying the numbers back and forth to one another.

But we need to consider abortion just enough to see whether we would be ready to choose this route were we to be pregnant. If we have sex and become pregnant, and if we cannot imagine choosing to raise the child or placing the child for adoption, then either we are ready to choose an abortion, or we need to do everything we possibly can to avoid becoming pregnant. So, what would it mean to choose an abortion?

One thing it means is addressing this issue of whether ending the life that is in the womb is "murder," in which case, of course, none of us would do it. This question is one of the numbered ones we might have mentioned above: *What is the status of the fetus?* and *When does life begin?* are part of our common vocabulary. Remember that Mark and Tami also faced some tension at this level of decision making, as they initially had differences of opinion on whether to have the abortion. Finally, Tami raised the issue of how she would feel in the future if she had the abortion; she decided she would harbor guilt for the rest of her life and would never feel confident she had done the right thing. In trying to discover whether we could have an abortion, then, let's look at these questions, the first one in an extended way, the others very briefly.

1. When does life begin?

For many, this is *the* question when it comes to abortion. In the minds of some, life begins at conception, so abortion is murder. In the minds of others, life begins at some other place—at the moment when twinning can no longer occur, or when the first brain waves appear, or at viability (when the life could survive on his or her own), for example—and this is the point past which abortion should not occur. Woven in among these different points of view are two different starting places: Some believe that God decides or has decided when life begins, so that a "right to life" is built into the structure of reality, while others believe that society must decide when it will regard life as having begun or when it will bestow such a right. From these starting points, the various positions try to sort out the issue of when the life in the womb should or must be treated as having the same value as life outside the womb.

Frankly, this debate is a philosophical and theological quagmire. Since the literature attempting to sort it out is vast, and you can easily consult it, let's see if we can help ourselves make at least a bit of progress by taking a slightly different path. As of conception, what is in the uterus is a *form* of human life. After all, biologically speaking, the fertilized egg is alive (it is neither dead nor inanimate, since it grows), and if it develops well and fully, it will become what we all recognize as a human being, not an oak tree or a bison or a supercomputer.

As we saw in the first chapter, we consider it a basic assumption of our lives that human life is not to be harmed; that's how we navigate our world. But, and here's where it gets tricky, this is not an absolute principle. Some of us believe in capital punishment and war and self-defense, for example, which are places where we take harm to others to be acceptable, for a variety of reasons. We also know that sometimes we have to harm people in order to make them better, such as when we cut someone open to perform surgery. And we all know that harm sometimes just happens, as in natural disasters or when we fall down on an icy sidewalk. The point here is simply that harm, intentional and unintentional, with results we consider to be good and results we consider to be bad, is part of our world. We seek to minimize it, but there are some times when we consider it appropriate.

This leads us to restate our question. What we really want to know is not when life begins, but under what conditions particular kinds of intentional harm to various forms of life are acceptable. Specifically, under what conditions is the intentional harm of killing the form of human life in the womb permissible? Of course, as with all questions of this sort, this one comes with an implied "Why?" *What are the reasons* that killing this form of human life is never or always or sometimes morally acceptable?

Certainly, there are ways in which this question is no less perplexing than the question of when life begins or when the fetus is a "person." But it seems to have the advantage of raising for us an issue in which we are all interested and in which we all have a stake. When others may and may not be intentionally harmed is key to our legal system and many of our biggest moral dilemmas. If it helps to pose one question that we can all wrestle with, perhaps ours has an advantage over something such as "When does life begin?" or "Is the fetus a person?"

2. Who makes the decision?

The quick answer is that the two who created the pregnancy make the decision, with a deciding vote given to the woman in whose body this form of human life is growing. That quick answer is often easier in theory than in practice, as once again the quality of your relationship comes into play. It is easy to find situations where a woman had an abortion against the wishes of her partner and situations where she did not have an abortion even though her partner encouraged it. In the end, as we said, that is her legal right and, as someone must make the final decision in these cases, her moral right as well. As you think about having sex, it can be worth pondering whether your prospective sexual partner is someone you would trust to join you in trying to make a good decision.

3. How would you feel?

Elizabeth said in the story about her first pregnancy scare that she thought having an abortion would make her feel guilty. In her second story, she used the language of "devastated." We just saw above that Tami felt she would also wonder whether she had done the right thing. Sometimes with abortion, if the feelings are troubling or negative ones, we may not be able to find a way to let them go, or so friends have told me about their own feelings. Of course, many of the feelings that can come with having an abortion can be, at least in the end, positive, for we may deeply believe that we made the best and right decision. The point here is simply for you to explore who you are a bit and see if you can discover what you might feel if you had an abortion. Does that, then, tell you anything about whether or not you want to have sex?

This chapter has been filled with complex and often emotionally charged stories and issues. If you do not have sex until you are ready to welcome children into the world, many of the issues discussed here may seem pretty theoretical to you. On the other hand, if you are planning on having sex but have yet to explore some of the issues related to pregnancy and birth control, I hope this chapter and the previous one will be helpful to you in beginning that process. What do you think at this moment: How does the possibility of unplanned pregnancy affect your reflections on sex?

Questions for Reflection and Discussion

1. Have you ever been pregnant or impregnated a sexual partner? What were the circumstances in which that pregnancy occurred? What choices did you make? How do you feel about them today?
2. I offered one possible way to think about the issue of fetal life in this chapter. Does it seem to you to be a helpful way to try to make sense of this key to the abortion debates?
3. This and the previous chapter try to present a certain "logic" concerning sex, pregnancy, and birth control. Does this logic make sense to you? Why or why not?
4. You have completed thinking about five puzzle pieces at this point. Where do you stand on the larger question of whether or not to have sex?

Chapter 6

Have You Made Any Promises?

*W*e surround our sexual activity with promises. We promise God, our parents, our friends, or ourselves that we won't have sex until we are married or have met our "one true love." We promise partners that we will be exclusive. We wake up in the morning and promise ourselves that we will never do again what we did the night before. We promise God, our spouses-to-be, and a gathered congregation that we will be faithful "until death do us part." When a friend worries that sex will change our relationship, we promise that it won't. Perhaps it is the vulnerability of sex that makes it an area of life where promises are so important. Perhaps these promises and the commitments they entail are one of the ways we try to stay safe in an unpredictable world.

In this chapter, we will first look at four general features of promises. These will give us a more complete understanding of the power of promises and the act of promising. Then we will draw on some of these ideas to examine promises to others, promises to ourselves, and promises to God as we ponder our sixth puzzle piece, represented by the question, What promises have you made that are relevant to your decision to have sex?

Four General Features of Promises

The promises we make and the promises made to us help us to define our relationships and our world. This first general feature of promises reminds us of the power they have in our lives. From what may be relatively small things, such as an auto shop's promise to have my car ready by noon or my promise to pick up my wife's favorite peanut butter on my way home, to relatively big things, such as a father's promise to pick up his child as soon as school is dismissed or an insurance company's promise to pay for a needed medical procedure or my promise to myself to quit smoking, promises play significant roles in defining our lives. During one particularly difficult time in my life, a friend who had stopped by for a visit left my house with the words "Anytime, anywhere." I could tell that this was not a throwaway line but a heartfelt promise, one he has kept. Hearing that promise in those moments meant a great deal to me, for it meant that I was not as alone in the world as I had been feeling. The promise has helped to shape my world and my relationship with my friend for many years.

Second, promises require trust. Because promises, which are about the future, cannot be proven in the present to be in any way fulfilled, we must place a significant amount of trust in other people when we rely on their promises never to cheat on us (something we can never know for sure) or always to treat us with love. Our inability to know the future is one of the reasons that we often want to know someone well before we become sexually intimate with her or him; we need to build up trust.

Our third feature of promises is that they may be explicit or implicit. Explicit promises include the "I'll be there" said by a friend whom we ask to help us move into a new apartment over the weekend, our signature on a contract that says we will buy a house for a certain price, or the notation on our driver's license that pledges we will be an organ donor. Other promises are implicit, such as the one each of us makes to his or her neighbor to "live and let live," or the promises I make to someone simply by virtue of the fact that I am his or her close friend. Both implicit and explicit promises will be important when we begin thinking about the role of promises in our sexual relationships.

Finally, not keeping promises can be injurious, depending in part on the significance of the promise. If you are eager to get into medical school, and you believe someone's promise that the Medical College Admission Test (MCAT) is simple and there is no reason to study for it, your hopes of attending the school of your dreams could well be dashed. For another example, I may feel deeply betrayed and angry if I arrive home to find that the trusted neighbor I have hired to babysit is making out with his girlfriend on the front porch while my children are inside the house playing with matches. In these two cases (an explicit promise that a test is easy and an implicit promise to take good care of my children) the promises might have gone awry in two different ways. It could be that the "promises" were lies to begin with: the person talking to you about the MCAT knew the test was difficult, and my neighbor had no intention of watching my children. Or it could be that there were no intentions to deceive, but, for good or bad reasons, the promises were not kept. However we make sense of the particular instances, one false or unkept promise may damage a relationship, while many can pull apart a society.

Keeping these features of promises in mind as the background of our discussion, we will look here at promises we make to others, promises we make to ourselves, and promises we make to God, with a brief concluding section on promises a proposed sexual partner has made that are relevant to whether one will choose to have sex with her or him. We will be guided through major portions of our discussion by reflecting on portions of the history of a woman named Rebecca. Here are some questions to ponder: What do you see in her story that is or is not important for your own life? As you ponder how your decision to have sex is influenced by the shape of this sixth puzzle piece, how are you doing with the promises in your life? Are you keeping promises about having sex that you have made in the past? When you make promises about choices you have made in the past, are they accurate? Are you making promises about the future that you truly intend to keep? Finally, are you acting in concert with the decisions you have made earlier in this exploration about how you will treat other people?

Promises to Others

You have undoubtedly made many promises to other people so far in your life, and some of you have made promises to others that concern sexual behavior of one sort or another. Maybe you promised to be exclusive in your sexual activity with a girlfriend or boyfriend. Maybe you did not promise to be exclusive with your primary partner, but you promised always to use a condom if you have oral, vaginal, or anal sex with anyone else. You might have promised to go on the pill so that you could begin having sex with a particular person soon. You might have promised to be tested for one or another STI. Perhaps you told your girlfriend or boyfriend that you were not ready to have sex yet, but you promised you would have sex with her or him one day soon. Maybe you promised that you would keep the details of your sexual relationship private, even if you did not last as a couple. One dimension of the current puzzle piece is calling to mind any promises you have made and considering how they currently apply in your life. As you do this, we'll look at four questions:

1. Is it only harmful consequences that make it wrong not to keep promises?
Here's part of Rebecca's story to get us started with our first question:

> With all my boyfriends I made promises to be faithful. At the beginning of my college career I went back on this promise. I cheated on a boyfriend a

number of times, and each time I promised I would not do it again, and yet I always did. Thinking back on why I did this, I think we feel like when we get into relationships these days we have to be exclusive immediately. The best promise for a new couple to make is one of respect in which the two people promise to be honest with one another about their needs and wants.

Rebecca slept with a boyfriend, promising him that she would be faithful, then cheated on him by sleeping with someone else. She then promised herself that she would not cheat again, a promise she did not keep. We noted in this chapter's first section that harm is one frequent consequence of broken promises. Rebecca experienced some of this when she felt guilty about her cheating, and we can imagine that her boyfriend, Tyler, also felt some pain and betrayal when she finally told him the truth. In order to get at our first question here, let's change Rebecca's story in a couple of ways. Let's suppose she did not feel guilty, that she did not tell her boyfriend, and that, for whatever reason, there was no way he could ever find out. Let's also suppose we can eliminate any risk of pregnancy or STIs from the picture. If there are, then, no harmful consequences to Rebecca's cheating, would we still want to say that she did something wrong by breaking her promise?

I think we would. Let's try to put ourselves in Tyler's shoes for a moment. Presumably, Tyler cares enough about his relationship with Rebecca to want her to be faithful to him, so it seems as though he recognizes that he is risking something in being intimate with her. He is being vulnerable, emotionally and physically, and he is doing this on the condition of her fidelity. He cannot ever know whether she is cheating, as we have stipulated, but he takes that risk and trusts that she is not. Rebecca's action, then, appears to be wrong simply because it is a violation of Tyler's trust, which also forces him to base his actions with and feelings toward her on a lie or series of lies. What do you think about this? It is pretty clear that when breaking a promise causes harm, the damage done causes us to say that breaking the promise was wrong. Yet here there could be no obvious damage, and still I'm suggesting that most of us would say breaking the promise is wrong. Maybe that is because we think there *could* be damage, but I think it is more the case that we believe it is wrong to make people base their lives on lies, just as we do not want to be forced to base our own lives on lies. If this assumption is correct, then keeping promises would seem to be right based simply on the act of promising itself, regardless of what happens later. That's an important feature of promises to keep in mind, as it challenges any sense we might have along the lines of "Oh well, no one will ever find out, so breaking this promise isn't so bad."

Before we leave Rebecca's story for two other scenarios, we should note her analysis. Maybe she is just trying to excuse her cheating, but she suggests a culture, parallel to the "hook-up culture" about which so much has been written, in which exclusivity is demanded right away. People are seen spending a bit of time to get to know one another or going on what used to be called a "date," and they are a couple. It is intriguing to speculate about whether being forced into couples so quickly makes it more likely that people will cheat as part of the otherwise normal process of seeing who is their best "match." If this is the case, it might tell us something about how we want to proceed in our romantic lives.

2. How do implicit promises to others get made?

Let's consider another scenario. Tara and Nathan have been dating for seven months. They have spent many nights together, have engaged in mutual masturbation, and have shared oral sex, but they have not had intercourse. Indeed, neither of them has had sex before, and they told one another during the first week of their relationship that they wanted to have sex with only one person in life, namely, the person they married. They have not discussed this since that time, but they have always stopped short of intercourse in their sexual expression. One night, as they are being intimate with one another, Nathan, knowing that Tara has been on the pill for years in order to regulate her menstrual cycle, suggests that they have intercourse, and Tara agrees. They have sex. Has Nathan just expressed his intention to spend his life with Tara? Has Tara promised the same to Nathan? Put yourself in Tara's or Nathan's place, and decide whether you would think you were making a lifelong promise or one was being made to you in this case.

Situations such as this one can be a communication nightmare. Imagine the next morning. Nathan and Tara are snuggling, and Tara says, "Would you like to spend a couple of hours looking at rings today?" Perplexed, Nathan stutters something like, "Huh?" Over the next five uncomfortable minutes, it becomes clear that Tara believed Nathan was promising to be with her forever, as the one person she ever had sex with, and Nathan, having changed his mind about the whole "one partner for life" thing, assumed Tara must have changed her mind, too. Otherwise, she would not have said yes to having sex with him. Tara thought this was a sexy, private way to get preengaged; Nathan likes things just the way they are, with some extra sex added in. The entire, sad story reminds us that people assume promises are made in a number of ways and that being explicit about what we are and are not promising can eliminate a lot of possible misunderstanding and pain.

3. Can the social context in which we live create promises we are responsible for keeping?

Here's a situation aimed at helping us ponder this question. Jeff and Molly met three hours ago. They have been having a wonderful time dancing and talking, though they have not talked about sex. Molly invites Jeff to her apartment, where they make out and have sex without a condom but still without having any conversation about sex or about their relationship. Have any promises been made here? For example, as twenty-first-century, educated people, has their having sex without a condom implicitly made the promises that (1) Molly is on the pill or otherwise protected against unplanned pregnancy and (2) neither Jeff nor Molly has an STI? In a social context where all of us know that birth control and condoms are important, would it make sense for Jeff and Molly to awaken in the morning and be worried about pregnancy or disease? If Molly becomes pregnant, would she be correct in expecting Jeff to partner with her in planning how to handle the pregnancy, based simply on the fact that he is an intelligent, twenty-first-century man who knows how pregnancy occurs? Would Jeff be right in supposing that if Molly becomes pregnant, she will call him so that he can share in the decision making about the future? Are Molly and Jeff making implicit promises to one another as educated people having sex in a society whose sexual challenges are well known?

4. Does merely having sex with someone make promises to him or her?

This is very similar to the question above, but it is less about social context and more about the fact of sex itself. Or, since those two are not fully separable, we might ask the more specific question of whether the fact that sex brings with it emotional and physical vulnerability entails promises on the part of the couple involved in it. Here is how one person answered the question.

> I think that there is an implicit promise when you are sexual with someone. Whether the two people recognize it or not, being sexual is a very vulnerable experience, and you are trusting that the other person will be caring and loving with your body. There is a promise that the sexual actions that are about to be engaged in will not be harmful to either of the partners, and that the goal for each person is to be caring and loving to the other person.
>
> When it comes down to it, all promises should be explicit where sex is concerned. All promises should be thought out and discussed, because only then will they become effective and meaningful guides in the decision process for being sexual.

It should be clear, at this point, how important some of these questions can be in trying to figure out whether to have sex. We are just over halfway through this chapter; have you reached any conclusions about what promises have a claim on your sexual activity at this moment in your life and context?

Promises to Self

A friend and I were leaving a conference one day several years ago. As we were reflecting on the accommodations, I asked him whether he had watched any of the "adult" movies that were available in his room (and, for the record, I hadn't). He said no, that this was not who he wanted to be. Leaving aside the issue of whether watching adult movies is a good or bad thing to do, I want to highlight this notion of the kind of person we want to be, for pondering it seems to me to be an important source of our promises to ourselves. Let's keep this in mind as we look at another piece of Rebecca's story. Remember that Rebecca had cheated on her boyfriend multiple times, felt guilty about it, and finally confessed.

> Later in college was the time I started really thinking for myself, and that's when I promised myself that I would only have vaginal intercourse with someone with whom I was in love. With my next boyfriend, maybe because I was afraid that he would leave me if I didn't have sex with him, or maybe because I just wanted to have sex and figure out what the big deal was, I remember lying in bed with him and knowing that I just wanted to do it. So I convinced myself that I loved him and told him I wanted to have sex. I don't remember anything about the actual act of vaginal intercourse that night; I just remember that I had to keep telling myself that I loved him because I didn't want to break that promise to myself. Later, though, I walked back to my dorm, all the while knowing that I didn't love him. For weeks I felt guilty, and I would like to say that I stopped having sex with him, but I didn't until months later. I believed that once I had sex, the promise to myself was broken and I couldn't get it back. But eventually I realized that this wasn't what I wanted sex to be, and that the one promise I really do value is waiting to have sex until I am in a loving relationship.

One way to try to understand Rebecca's thoughts and actions here is to say that who she wants to be, her "true self," is not in accord with the person she is being in the world. It takes a number of years for her to figure out that she only wants to be having sex with someone she loves and who loves her, so then when she has sex for other reasons, she tells herself that the relationship must be a loving one. The tension between who she wants to be and the way she is living, however, is a tension she feels constantly, in this case in the form of guilt.

There is nothing unusual in Rebecca's situation. Most of us have images of ourselves that do not always mesh with the way we act. Indeed, one of the ways we typically become the person we want to be is by noticing these places of tension and working hard to overcome them. We may not think of ourselves as the sort of person who cheats on an exam, but then we cheat. We may think of ourselves as a kind person, but then we ignore someone in need. It is difficult to face these conflicts in ourselves, but one of the ways we try to do so is by making promises to ourselves. Rebecca promised again and again that she would have sex only with someone with whom she was in a loving relationship; that promising was not enough to motivate her, however, until she got angry at her sexual partner and broke away from him.

Different strategies will work for different people as we face these tensions, but one thing we want to try to avoid is self-deception. It is very easy to absolve ourselves quickly from promises we make by saying that we just haven't quite caught up with our true self yet. Forgiving ourselves is surely important, but so is facing the tough struggles of trying to live life as we choose and not whichever way our random desires and inclinations lead us. Someone who was involved in a 12-step program once told me that we can't always think our way into a new way of acting but must act our way into a new way of thinking. That seems right to me. Sometimes, we simply have to force ourselves to act in the way we deeply know is right and best, the way that is our best self, until we have minimized the temptation to go in the other direction.

A good friend, let's call her Judy, once acted in a way that was incompatible with her "true self," her personal values. She was on her own for the first time, living in a new city and working in a new career. Always a very studious person in school, she had promised herself that she was going to try new things and live a little. However, when she woke up in a near-stranger's bed one morning after a night of alcohol and what she considered to be bad decisions, she was extremely upset. Her behavior did not fit with her view of herself. Put another way, she violated implicit promises to herself.

If we think of Judy's true self, the Judy she wanted to be, the Judy who had taken shape over the decades of her life, as a collection of promises to herself about how she would and would not act, we can see her one-night stand as being "out of character." It was not true to herself; it did not fit implicit promises she had made to herself through her decades of life, promises to respect herself and to demand respect from others, promises not to put herself in harm's way or take unnecessary risks, promises to be cared about when she gave herself sexually to someone. Eventually, this led Judy to make some explicit promises to herself about how she would act in the future, promises that were to have great positive impact on her in the several years between this event and her marriage.

What promises have you made to yourself? Have you made implicit ones, such as Judy's that she was not a one-night-stand person? Have you made explicit ones, such as Rebecca's that she only wanted to have sex with someone she loved? How do these influence the way you are thinking about your current decision about having sex?

Promises to God

Here is another part of Rebecca's story:

> My mom told me that God gave me this beautiful body and out of love and respect for God, I should value my body and only give it to the man I marry. In this way I did make a promise to God. The problem with my making a promise with God at that time in my life is that I didn't have a clear understanding of God. I found that it is difficult to make a promise to just the word "God," and therefore it was easy for me to break this promise, which I did.

In addition to explicit and implicit promises to ourselves and to others, there are implicit and explicit promises to God. We can make promises directly to God, such as telling God we will not have sex until we are married. We can make promises that are not explicitly to God but are implicit in other aspects of our relationship with God. And, with God, there is also a third kind of promise. We can make promises before or in the presence of God, so that our intention is to include God as a witness to the promise and, we hope, as an enabler of its fulfillment. Marriage vows are often seen as this kind of promise, a covenant not only between husband and wife but between husband, wife, and God. God is not a disinterested observer here but a participant in the covenant between the two people; in a parallel way, the "witnesses" are also participants and, in other parts of such services, pledge their support and prayers to and for the married couple.

Because there are intentions attached to them, *explicit* promises to God and before God are reasonably easy to identify in our lives. If you promise faithfulness to your spouse in a Christian marriage ceremony, God is understood to be in one or another sense a third party in the promise, binding the two of you together and sustaining you in the journey of life together. If you say directly to God when you get out of bed the morning after a casual hookup that you will never do that again, and you mean it (as opposed to its being a mere expression of exasperation with yourself: "God, I'll never do *that* again."), then you have made a promise to God.

Implicit promises to God, on the other hand, are more difficult to ponder, but, again, a scenario will be helpful. Carrie goes to church a couple of times each month. If asked, she will say that she believes in God and in the traditional creeds of the Christian faith. She prays at church and at some point during most days, usually asking God to help people she knows are having a difficult time in some way. She tries to love her neighbor in her daily life, and she volunteers in one of the church's service projects a few times each year. Has Carrie, through her religious behavior, made implicit promises to God about her sex life? It seems so. Carrie expresses and seeks to strengthen her relationship with God through her Christian life. Most Christians believe that this God with whom they relate has something to say to them about life, even sexual life. Part of being in this relationship is committing oneself to hearing and following God. It makes sense then to say of anyone who seriously identifies himself or herself as a Christian, and acts in ways appropriate to that identification, that he or she has promised to live in accordance with God's view on sex, whatever those views may be. This may be seen as a promise to oneself and a promise to other Christians, but it is also a promise to God, who lies at the center of the Christian life. This is not an easy notion to wrap our minds around, but if we remember that any committed relationship is likely to bring with it implicit promises, it should be easy enough to make sense of these implicit promises to God.

Rebecca faces a troubling discovery when she finds that she no longer believes in the God to whom she made her promise. This may or may not be the position most of you reading this book are in, but it is certainly not unusual that we find our understandings of God changing over the years. In what kind of God would we need to believe in order for it to make sense to make promises to God? We would need a God who in some sense hears and understands us, perhaps a God who will support us in trying to act in one way rather than another, and also a God who wants a relationship with us and with whom we want a relationship. We'll reflect more on God and sex in the next chapter, but here it simply seems important to realize that making promises to God requires having an idea of God that makes this action make sense. What is your view of God, and how does this connect with your view of making promises?

Care for the Promises of the Other

If you have been working on the many issues in this chapter and how they pertain to your own life and sexual decisions, you may be quite tired of thinking about promises. I ask you to bear with me, though, for just one additional question: Do we have any responsibility to help our prospective sexual partners keep their promises? If Alan knows that Kathy is trying to understand how God would have her live, but she seems willing to have sex with him after the party tonight, does he have any responsibility to raise the God issue with her? If Kathy heard Alan say to one of his friends that he is never going to hook up again, because he always feels so ashamed of himself, but he seems willing to hook up with her, does she have any responsibility to talk with him about this? These questions are simply intended to start you thinking about some of the ways the various puzzle pieces we are exploring might overlap. How should I treat the promises others have made if I have decided not to harm others, to foster good, or to love my neighbor? What do you think?

Questions for Reflection and Discussion

1. Are there times when it is appropriate to break promises? Is it ever the right thing to do, or is it simply forgivable?
2. We saw this quotation earlier in the chapter: "I think that there is an implicit promise when you are sexual with someone. Whether the two people recognize it or not, being sexual with someone is a very vulnerable experience, and you are trusting that the other person will be caring and loving with your body. There is a promise that the sexual actions that are about to be engaged in will not be harmful to either of the partners, and that the goal for each person is to be caring and loving to the other person's body." Do you agree or disagree? Why?
3. Have you ever made a nonsexual promise to God? Did you learn anything about God or your understanding of God through doing that?
4. We said at the beginning of the chapter that we surround ourselves with promises because sex makes us so vulnerable. What does it mean to you to be vulnerable? Does making or receiving promises address that vulnerability in a helpful way?
5. What is the last sexual promise, implicit or explicit, that you made? Have you kept it? Why or why not? What did the process tell you about who you really are?
6. How can we learn to make our implicit promises explicit? Should we always do that?

Chapter 7

What Do God and the Bible Offer?

When exploring any of life's important moral issues, Christians want to know what God thinks. If God supports Christians' going to war in some cases, then perhaps it is time for us to enlist. If God doesn't like hypocrisy, then maybe we need to say less about the evils of capitalism and do more to help those who are poor. Where does God stand on such things? Does God have a view on capital punishment, violent sporting events, public options for health care, in vitro fertilization, pornography, how we earn our income, or what we do and do not eat? For Christians and many others who believe in God, God's view is the right view, so knowing God's view enables us to know how we should live.

The same reasoning applies to a decision about having sex. Does God think it's okay for young, single people to have sex? Is it only okay, in God's eyes, if they are engaged or in love? Does God approve of having sex with one partner this weekend and another partner next weekend, as long as no one is hurt in the process? If we accept the idea that we should implement God's wishes for our lives, it becomes very important for us to attempt to discern what it is that God thinks about our puzzle. But how do we do that? How can we discover in which direction God would have us go?

To begin to answer this question, we will explore two sides to our seventh puzzle piece. The first will raise the question of whether thinking about God in one way rather than another might lead us to different conclusions about having sex. For this part of our puzzle piece, you are invited to ponder how you understand God and whether this understanding shapes your view of unmarried sex. The second side to this puzzle piece requires us to look at the ways in which Christians claim to know what it is God thinks about things. We will pay attention to four of these ways, spending most of our time on the Bible as a primary source for Christian reflection on God and sex.

Before tackling the two sides of this puzzle piece, we should address one other issue. At this point, it would be reasonable for you to have the impression that this chapter would only be relevant for Christians and perhaps others who believe in God or gods. This would be a mistaken impression, however, so we should say just a couple of things about why this puzzle piece is not only for religious people.

Why This Puzzle Piece Is Not Only for People of Religious Faith

This puzzle piece is for everyone. That may seem like an odd claim, given the title of the chapter, but there are at least two good reasons why people of every faith and people of no particular religious faith should be concerned with the issue that Christians articulate as the relevance of God to sexual behavior. First, any time something we do or a way we live has an impact on others, everyone has a stake in our behavior and the ideas that shape it. Christian ideas about God shape both Christian sexual behavior, which has a public dimension (see chapter 9), and the public stands Christians take on issues related to sex and sexuality. So everyone, not just Christians, has a vested interest in what Christians do sexually and in the ideas on which they ground their sex-related decisions. These ideas flow from the Bible and other sources we will explore below.

The second reason everyone has a stake in evaluating Christian views on God and God's relevance to sex is because of the *role* or *function* of ideas of God in the Christian life. For Christians and others who believe in God, the idea of God functions to orient us beyond ourselves to that which is permanent, whole, and good. It enables us to locate ourselves in the world and to begin to make sense of who we are. However, the search to make sense of things is not only a Christian or religious search; it is a human search. Those who do not believe in God typically find alternative ideas or values around which to orient their lives (examples might include the search for truth, kindness to others, the accumulation of wealth, the well-being of family, or the preservation of the self). For those of us who find our orientation somewhere other than in God, therefore, our seventh puzzle piece concerns the appropriateness of the ideas or values that sit at the core of our lives and the ways that these ideas and values shape our decisions about sex. When the term "God" or related language appears in the chapter, then, you might choose to replace it with the phrase "the idea of God," or a different articulation of orienting values, reminding yourself in that way that you are assessing the relevance of core values to sexual life. Although I will not stop to point this out at every turn, our goal is to identify and assess the life-orienting ideas, Christian or otherwise, that shape our decisions about sex.

Who God Might Be (and Why It Matters)

We said above that the first part of this seventh puzzle piece calls on us to consider whether different ways of thinking about God might lead us to different conclusions about having sex. To ponder this, let's look at some of the ways Christians understand God and then ask whether any of these might lead to or be more compatible with certain views on sex rather than others. If for purposes of this discussion we define Christians as people who seek to orient their lives around the God who is revealed in the Old and New Testaments of the Bible and in the church's ongoing relationship with Jesus Christ, then the views of God that emerge from these places are those we are considering. These views vary greatly, as three admittedly impressionistic illustrations will suggest. The first might be called an educated guess on my part; the second is a look at answers to a question I posted on Facebook some time ago; and the third is simply a report from the introductory theology classes I teach regularly.

First, here is my educated guess from talking with people about these things over the last several decades. I imagine that if we were to ask a dozen Christians how they describe God, the odds are pretty good that some of these words would be among the first ones we would hear: *creator, savior, spirit, love, loving, lover, father, righteous, just, protector, triune, all-powerful, all-knowing, all-good, present, mysterious, gracious, holy, friend, perfect, judge, lawgiver.* Many Christians, on hearing or reading this list, would be likely to affirm not only a few but all of these terms as characterizing the God in whom we believe.

For my second illustration of varying views of God among Christians, let's turn to Facebook. In pondering ideas for this book, I put four questions on my Facebook page and invited my friends to respond to them. One of those questions was whether and how our sexual thinking or activity might be informed by our faith. Here are brief excerpts from five of the many responses I received.

> [My] surrounding culture treats [sex] profanely. It's hard not to be influenced by these other voices, especially when my body and my TV run at a higher volume than God's whispers.

The way I approach sex is that, as God's creation, I should honor him, honor myself, and honor my partner (who is also a creation of God).

I've learned that sex is a way for me to strengthen my connection with my partner, and that strengthens our connection to God.

I think God must be proud of inventing sex, and God must be pleased when two people love each other as much as [we] love each other. . . . I also believe that sex helps us understand God's love.

I believe that my God wants me to be happy, to be educated and to know what I want out of life. . . . I feel that God wants us to know ourselves and to make the best, healthiest decisions that we can.

These quotations illustrate the reasonably common Christian confidence that God is somehow relevant to our sex lives. This confidence is expressed, however, with a number of different images of God. The first friend offers the idea that God's voice can be heard but can be very quiet. The second notes that God has created each of us and that God should be honored. My third friend suggests a God who connects with us in part by way of our connection with others. The fourth friend recognizes a God who loves us, has created sex, and has the capacity to be pleased by the behavior of human beings; presumably, though the author does not say this, such a God could also be displeased. Finally, my fifth friend tells us that God wants us to be happy and to make good decisions for our lives. It could well be that any or all of the five authors represented by these excerpts would agree with all five of the images of God just mentioned, but these excerpts from what they have said emphasize different elements of God's nature and activity.

My third and final illustration of varying Christian views on God stems from my experiences in teaching introductory theology classes. Many of the Christians in these classes are confident that God is somehow relevant to their sexual beliefs and practices, as with all of their moral choices, though they fall into two widely different camps on the nature of that relevance. I have no idea, of course, whether what they say actually reflects or shapes the ways in which they live, but the two most typical responses among those who self-identify as Christians are as follows:

1. God, through the Bible or the church or our conscience, tells us what we should be doing and not doing. In this case, God says not to have sex until we're married, so we shouldn't have sex until we're married.
2. Neither the Bible nor the church is really trustworthy for providing moral guidelines in the contemporary world, but Jesus told us to love one another, and we should follow that principle, no matter what else we do.

These are obviously rather different views of how to live sexually and also of how to read the Bible and understand church traditions, but, most importantly for our exploration, they appear to entail rather different views of God. In the first instance, we have what sounds like God as giver of laws or specific rules, who has told us precisely, at least on some issues, what we should and should not do. In the second case, God sounds more like a friend or giver of a broad principle for life, who calls us to love one another, whatever else we decide to do. The two views of God accompany two views of when sex is appropriate: the first group thinks Christians should wait until marriage to have sex, while the second sees that as only one of many legitimate possibilities.

Okay, so we Christians are anything but univocal in the ways we articulate God's nature and activity, including the relevance of God to our sexual behavior. So what? What is the importance of this recognition for how we respond to this puzzle piece? To exaggerate our answer a bit, the first thing we say to the question of what God thinks we should do sexually is to ask, Which God? Are we talking about the lawmaking God, who hands us rules and expects us to follow them to the letter? Are we referring to the God who just wants us to love one another, whatever else we do? Could we mean the lover God of the mystics, with whom we can be so intimate that our descriptions sound like sex? Are we talking about the Creator God, who has made us sexual in the first place and perhaps instilled meaning into our sexual lives? Could we mean the Father God, who expects our obedience, or the God who sets us free to make our own good and bad decisions? Or perhaps our God is the God of mystery, whose ways really cannot be known much at all. These are different ways of thinking about God (or different versions of the *idea* of God) and different ways of thinking about God's relationship to our sexual lives. At any given time, even if all of these ways of seeing God are ultimately compatible, some of us will see different images of God as primary, and these primary images will influence the ways we see God's role in our sexual lives.

If, then, you are a Christian, you might start constructing your seventh puzzle piece by identifying the primary ways you think of God. List four or five of them. If you think there is a connection between God and our moral lives or, in particular, between God and our sexual lives, how would you explain or define it? Does it fit better with some of your ways of understanding God than with others? All you are attempting to do here is to put yourself in a position to evaluate your understanding of God and your current sense of when to have sex and, in cases where these two do not seem to fit together well, to ponder which one you might need to examine more closely. A short time of reflection on this issue can give you helpful clarity on the role of God in your reflections on having sex.

If you think of yourself more as a humanist than a person of religious faith, you might well assess the implications for society of people holding some of the previously mentioned views of God rather than others. Are we better off with certain ideas about God all around us than with others? And what are the implications of your preferred views for the way the culture views sex? The other task you might well wish to take on is determining your own central values. What gets *you* out of bed in the morning? Around what commitments is your life centered? Do your values and commitments suggest that some views on sex will make more sense to you than others?

Where We Christians Get Our Ideas—Introduction

The first part of this seventh puzzle piece was trying to ascertain who God is for us and how that fits with our sense of what we should do sexually. This section of our chapter concerns the second part of this puzzle piece: where we Christians typically get our ideas about God and sex. We'll begin to ponder the nature of one of the four sources, the Bible, and we will discuss a bit of the content about sex that we might find in each source. Finally, we will raise the issue of how the sources might be weighed, prioritized, or balanced.

The moral lives of faithful Christians may look very different from one another, depending on the part of the Christian tradition to which they adhere and depending on the ways they understand and prioritize the primary sources for Christian theological reflection. These sources, collectively referred to as the "Wesleyan quadrilateral" because of their articulation by John Wesley, but expanded a bit here, might be stated this way: Christians in all times and places, seeking to know God and live faithfully, have drawn on (1) the Bible; (2) the religious thoughts and practices that were handed down to them (tradition); (3) rational thinking in general, the philosophical and scientific approaches that surrounded them, and what we would today call social-scientific data and analysis; and (4) their own experiences of life in Christ and human experience more generally. Let's take a look at what each one of these says about God's relevance for our sexual expression. As we go, you might ponder three questions: If you were to put these four sources in order, ranking the one from which you get most of your ideas about God and sex as number one and the one from which you get the fewest of your ideas as number four, what would the order be? Why do you prioritize the sources in this way? If you find these sources to be in conflict, how do you resolve the conflict?

Where We Christians Get Our Ideas—The Bible

In my experience, many Christians—including those who have definite ideas about its authority and content—have not actually read much of the Bible. Still, it is easy enough to argue that contemporary Christians are dependent on the Bible for their faith, either because they grew up in the church and heard it read and interpreted over and over, or because being a Christian today means being shaped by a set of texts that, had they been different, would have made contemporary expressions of the faith look quite different. The biblical texts and, another level back, the stories that they collect and develop are the foundation of Christian communities worldwide and the inspiration for the lives of millions of Christians, sometimes for better and sometimes for worse. Ultimately, whether firsthand or tenth hand, Christians know who God is and what God is doing because of the Bible.

Although this dependence of Christianity on the Bible means that Christians trying to understand themselves must at some point turn to the biblical texts, it does not require them to have a common understanding of what the Bible *is* and how it should be read. We will look at three different views on the Bible. The two we're about to see in this chapter might be considered the two ends of a Christian continuum on attitudes toward the Bible. One of the characters in chapter 11 will then offer a third approach. Your question in the end, of course, is whether you will adopt one of these views or some other, and why?

At one end of the continuum, some Christians describe the Bible as "God's Word," and they mean that in some way or other the Bible's words are God's words. The Bible, they say, is a unified text, so verses from one place may be used to illuminate verses from elsewhere. It is supernaturally revealed, and the Holy Spirit has ensured that it is free of errors. Christians can, therefore, trust what it says and live their lives accordingly. On the other end of the continuum are those Christians who think God may sometimes be seen or heard through the words of the Bible, but they do not believe the Bible's words are in any way God's direct words to us. Rather, they say, the Bible is a disparate collection of stories, experiences, and reflections of Jews and Christians who believed themselves to stand in special relationship with God, and all of these must be read using the tools of modern biblical criticism. Today's Christians can and should trust the value of some of the Bible's broad ideals (such as peace, love, and justice) as keys to faithful living, though even these must be assessed according to our own best understandings.

Let's look at just two of the passages in the Bible that concern sex, one from the Old Testament and one from the New Testament, and see how the ends of the continuum might understand them. The first of the two is Genesis

1–3, which is where the Bible's concern with sex appears to begin. In these opening chapters of the Bible's first book, God creates the world, including Adam and Eve, who sin in rejecting God's instructions and are consequently kicked out of the paradisiacal Garden of Eden. In the midst of these well-known passages occur sections that are taken to affirm the goodness of the physical world in general and of human bodies in particular, the importance of the complementarity of male and female, the norm of married life, the command to procreate, and the corruption of everything by Adam and Eve's disobedience. Here are a few verses from these chapters.

> So God created humankind in his image,
>   in the image of God he created them;
>   male and female he created them.
> God blessed them, and God said to them, "Be fruitful and multiply, and
>   fill the earth and subdue it;" . . .

Then the LORD God said, "It is not good that the man should be alone; I will make him a helper as his partner." . . . And the rib that the LORD God had taken from the man he made into a woman and brought her to the man. Then the man said,

> "This at last is bone of my bones
>   and flesh of my flesh;
> this one shall be called Woman,
>   for out of Man this one was taken."

Therefore a man leaves his father and his mother and clings to his wife, and they become one flesh. (Gen. 1:27–28a; 2:18, 22–25)

What might the "God's Word" end of the continuum say about this story? In their view, the verses mean that God created human beings as male and female, intending them to marry, to become "one flesh," and to procreate. These few verses shape the views of these Christians on, among other things, the relationship between husband and wife and the purpose of marriage. From the other end of the continuum, we would get a rather different response. In this view, the authors of the Genesis stories were giving their own society, composed of men and women coming together as husbands and wives to have and raise children, a divine meaning and origin. Whether we accept their understandings of relationships and structures as normative for us today depends in part, according to this end of the continuum, on whether such relationships and structures reflect our highest ideals and principles. Are they, for instance, loving and just?

Given Christians' focus on the New Testament, let's look at one passage from there. This is from one of the apostle Paul's letters.

> For this is the will of God, your sanctification: that you abstain from fornication; that each one of you know how to control your own body in holiness and honor, not with lustful passion, like the Gentiles who do not know God; that no one wrong or exploit a brother or sister in this matter, because the Lord is an avenger in all these things, just as we have already told you beforehand and solemnly warned you. For God did not call us to impurity but in holiness. Therefore whoever rejects this rejects not human authority but God, who also gives the Holy Spirit to you. (1 Thess. 4:3–8)

Those Christians who see the Bible as a unified text are more likely to read this passage through lenses that already accept the view, gathered in part from Genesis, that marriage is our norm and "fornication" ("sexual immorality," in the New International Version) and exploitation define or accompany sex outside of marriage. Christians more inclined to read the Bible through lenses of contemporary norms might see exploitation as the defining issue in this text. In this view, any sexual practices that exploit or use another person are "fornication" or sexual immorality, but sex between unmarried people, they are likely to argue, is not inherently exploitive.

If you want to know more about what the Bible says about sex, you can easily look up in a dictionary of the Bible or a concordance the various biblical passages that relate to sexual issues. The heart of the above discussion, however, is that we cannot avoid making choices about the lenses through which we read whatever passages we find. All Christians who claim to know anything about God and God's views on sex through their study of the Bible are reading it through some lens or other; there is no alternative. So would you choose one of the two lenses described here, or do you believe there are good reasons for choosing a different one, perhaps the one you will see in chapter 11? I have provided a couple of references on biblical interpretation in the book's Helpful Readings list that might help you explore the biblical text more fully.

Where We Christians Get Our Ideas—Tradition

Christians also claim to know something of who God is and what God is doing through the Christian tradition, seen both broadly and in the thousands of different shapes it has taken over the centuries. "Tradition" simply refers to those things that are handed down. For Christians, this includes widespread doctrines, such as the doctrine of the Trinity (the idea that God is three in one: Father, Son, and Holy Spirit), and widespread practices such as baptism in its many variations. It also includes variations in denominational understandings and practices of such things as ordination and variations in local understandings and practices of such things as tithing and Christian education. In all, the number of ways of living that are part of the Christian tradition is staggering.

We could ponder for a very long time all that the tradition has said about sex and having sex. We might, however, gain more from asking ourselves what we have each heard and not heard about sex from our own church traditions. Whether you are deeply committed to some collection of Christian beliefs and practices or you are a Christian who is best described as being in general sympathy with the main flow of the Christian story, you have probably seen evidence of attitudes toward sex at some point or other. If you are like many Christians, this "evidence" is an absence, and you have heard very little, and almost nothing positive, about sex, a tragedy that betrays the church's deep discomfort with dealing with issues of sexuality in a thoughtful and open way. On the other hand, you may have heard about the importance of reserving sex for marriage. You may have heard something about birth control and family planning and other related topics. You may have picked up on the tradition's valuing of the spirit over the body, which can have the consequence of either not talking about or talking only negatively about sex, especially in situations other than marriage. You may have heard claims and debates on one side or another of the current controversy about gay marriage. You may have heard cautions about divorce or adultery. You probably have not heard a lot about the joys and pleasures that can come with sex, unless perhaps you have heard a sermon or two on the celebratory Song of Songs. Not all of these few examples are deeply embedded in the tradition, though their roots probably are, but I offer them here simply as suggestions that might trigger your thinking as you reflect on how the Christian traditions involving sex have influenced your own life.

As before, whatever you find here calls for some assessment on your part. What do you see that you want to retain, and why? What do you see that you think is crazy, and why? Is what your tradition gives you the same as what you discovered in the Bible, and do you consider that to be a good or a bad thing? Here you are being invited, even challenged, to find where *you* stand and what *you* will commit yourself to, so what are your reasons for leaning toward or away from what you find in the Bible and your part of the Christian tradition?

Where We Christians Get Our Ideas—Reason

If you do not believe in God, then the Bible and the Christian tradition may not be sources you will ever draw on as resources on your sex life. The next two sources, though—reason and experience—are ones everyone should find helpful. As you read these next sections, consider what rational reflection, science, your own experiences, and the experiences of others you know offer for your own reflections on sex.

Critical thinking, philosophy, and science have contributed much to Christian thinking about God and what God is doing in the world, though this is not always easy to see, in part because reason is often placed over against faith in theological exploration. When that happens, reason is sometimes rejected for providing no insight worthy of Christian attention. But reason can be an important tool in understanding the Bible and discerning the best parts of the tradition. Indeed, faith is not opposed to reason but is instead a commitment to see the world in a particular way, a way discerned partly through reason. Let's look here at a parallel question to those we just posed in the sections on the Bible and on the tradition: What do Christians claim to know about God and sex through reason?

The current positions on each one of the issues mentioned in the previous section on tradition are the result of intensive rational reflection. The doctrine of the Trinity, for instance, was a conclusion of a series of arguments among leaders of the early church about the nature of God and the process of salvation. Decisions about whether infants or only adults should be baptized are a matter not of mere assertion but of rational reflection, and there are meaningful reasons given on both sides of the debate. The same would certainly be true of current understandings of the Eucharist. There are assumptions and "moves" in these various arguments that many people, Christian or not, would not make today, but that does not diminish the rationality of the arguments themselves.

An example of reason giving us some of our ideas about God and sex might come from traditional discussions about birth control. If we begin with the assumption that God created sex with procreation in mind, as many Christians have assumed over the centuries, then we might well end up with something like the modern Catholic prohibition against artificial birth control methods as apparently counter to God's will. When some late twentieth-century theologians attempted to replace the idea that every act of intercourse must be open to conception with the alternative idea that every marriage, as a whole, must be open to conception, it was partly a rational attempt to make more realistic a moral instruction that, in the eyes of many, flies in the face of modern economic and population realities, not to mention modern understandings of pleasure as a purpose of sex. Obviously, what we learn from these debates will depend upon our rationally guided decisions to stand in one place rather than another, but the arguments are clearly rational ones, both in the sense of being developed through critical thinking and in the sense of drawing upon scientific investigation of the world.

If you listen closely, you will find the tools and results of reason at work in discussions about abstinence education (e.g., what do statistics show about its effectiveness?), abortion (e.g., what is modern medicine able to tell us about the developmental stages of the fetus?), or arguments about the meanings of certain words in the biblical text (e.g., what has historical research told us about the connotations of some of the ancient words in texts that are apparently about homosexuality?). Can you find evidence of the use of reason, science, or data in your own thinking about sex up to this point? Where have you relied on rational thought and evidence, and where has something else taken precedence for you? If you were to weigh rational argument against church traditions and biblical teachings, which one would have priority for you, and why?

Where We Christians Get Our Ideas—Experience

Finally, what do Christians claim to know about God and sex through experience? That God is considered known through experience is very clear. When Jesus raised Lazarus from the dead, both Lazarus and all those who saw and heard the story learned about God through their experience. The women and then the disciples at the empty tomb of Jesus learned something of God through their experience. These not-yet-Christians saw clearly that God gives life. When the intercessory prayers of countless Christians through the ages were heard, when various spiritual disciplines brought renewed joy and friendship with God, when social justice movements were reinvigorated through worship and nonviolence, when a walk in the woods brought a peace that passed understanding, Christians said that they saw God at work, that they knew God or something specific about God through their experiences. This is still true today. Of all the ways Christians claim to find God or to have knowledge of God, experience is often the most personally powerful and transformative. Many of us have the attitude that we cannot believe what we do not personally experience, but when we do experience something, our interpretation of the experience can become so much a part of us that we assert its truth in the face of every possible kind of evidence to the contrary.

What of sex? What might Christians learn about God's view of our sex lives via experience? As always, the big issue here is that the answer can range from nothing at all to a whole lot, depending in part on the lenses with which we view our experiences. We could, of course, understand the guilt we feel after hooking up with someone as God's speaking to us or as parental programming. We can understand the pleasure we felt during an enjoyable sexual experience either as God's gift to us or as the presence of pleasure chemicals in our brain. One friend is very adamant that "sex is a unitive experience, that can be seen as mirroring the soul's frolicking with God." The experience of sex, for her, can be so intense and playful that it echoes the soul's playful encounters with God. Do we learn of God in these moments? Are there chemical explanations for these things? Are the two views compatible?

The experiences that tell us something of God's view of sex and of our sexual lives need not be personal ones; we often learn well from the experiences of others. If you use your lenses of faith on the Facebook quotations noted at the beginning of this chapter, what might you conclude about God's relationship to our sexual lives? Do you suppose, for example, that our sexual choices should honor God? Could you live by that view as a rule of life, only having sex if you can consciously honor God in your actions? What might we learn from pondering the horrible sexual experiences some people have? Could it be that our world is so broken (remember Adam and Eve and sin) that many of our sexual behaviors are far away from what God intended?

You can see the many kinds of questions we can raise and try to answer about the role of experience in helping us to discern how we should live sexually. In the end, of course, for Christians throughout history, no experience, no rational argument, no biblical text, and no tradition has stood alone as definitive of who God is and what God wants of us. Instead, Christians have tried to bring dimensions of all four of these sources together, sometimes quite intentionally and sometimes just as a deeply ingrained approach to God and life, to understand the world and our place in it. As a final exploration on our part, what do we do if we think two or more of these sources stand in tension, leaving us no clear answer?

Prioritizing and Reconciling Sources

Jesus appears to want to tighten up certain Old Testament practices when he announces that divorce is only permissible in cases of adultery. Parts of the Christian tradition have held that as a sign of God's unending faithfulness, Christian divorce does not make sense theologically and is sinful.

Experientially, many Christians have discovered that some marriages simply do not work, becoming loveless over time, and have experienced God as calling them to new life beyond their previous commitments. Other Christians have argued that abuse is a worse violation of a marriage than adultery and clearly justifies divorce, appealing not only to experience but to rational arguments about the consequences of abuse. You can see the tension in the various sources, even with this very brief description. How should we weigh the Bible's and the tradition's prohibition or near-prohibition of divorce against a frequently held contemporary view that some divorces are exactly what should happen for the emotional, spiritual, and even physical good of the two divorcing people? How should we understand very recent traditions of honoring the dissolution of marriage in a religious ceremony, making explicit the oftentimes implicit sense that God would honor this separating? If we cannot find a way to reconcile the sources and their ideas, what principles could we use to prioritize them? Should we appeal to typically Protestant views that put the Bible first? Should we try to use a broad principle like love, which has roots in all four sources? You can see here the challenges we face in trying to bring together or prioritize the various sources of what many consider to be God's wisdom on the issue of divorce.

These kinds of tensions exist when it comes to our central question of whether two unmarried people can justifiably have sex. Consider the Bible: First, we must recognize the tension in the biblical text itself, which seems to accept a cultural norm of sex within marriage yet contains no uncontroversial prohibition against sex between two unmarried people (though there are passages that can easily be taken to imply this). Second, even if there were such a prohibition, we must decide among the various approaches to interpreting the Bible. Which of the two we described, for instance, should we accept? Or would another approach be better?

Drawing on the tradition, we would have to say that the weight of the church's teachings have fallen on the side of the marriage norm, but we would have to weigh that against, among other things, a significant number of contemporary Christian thinkers who appear to be open to revising that norm. These thinkers will be among those who are viewed in coming years as part of the tradition of the church. Experientially, the fact that great faithfulness to God and love of neighbor often appear to walk hand in hand with unmarried sex at least raises the issue of whether unmarried sex really alienates one from God, as some think. Facts and statistics about STIs and the effects of pregnancy are among the scientific data that could be brought to bear on the negative side of unmarried sexual intercourse, though the development of safer and more reliable birth control can address one of those concerns. We also want to keep in mind the claims of some that sex, whether between married people or unmarried people, seems to reveal to them something of the nature and activity of God in their lives. On the whole, Christian arguments can be made both for and against the appropriateness of having sex when one is unmarried. Your question is which arguments are the *best*, and this book claims that answering that involves answering for yourself a number of important questions, including but not limited to your view of God's role in your sexual life.

If you have paused to answer even half of the questions in this chapter, you may well have taken an important theological journey. If you have followed the discussion while substituting language such as "the idea of God" for "God" and pondering the *kinds* of issues discussed here within your own framework of values and ways of making sense of the world, then you have taken an important philosophical journey. In either case, I hope you have discovered something about yourself that you didn't know before and that the shape you give to this seventh puzzle piece brings you closer to your conclusion about whether or not to have sex.

Questions for Reflection and Discussion

1. Now that you've spent some time thinking about the various sources for Christian knowing, would you prioritize them any differently than you said at the beginning of the chapter?
2. If you are a Christian, toward which end of the interpretive continuum do your views on the Bible lean? How does this shape your view of the role of sex in your life?
3. Which of the five views of God that showed up in response to my Facebook inquiry feels like something you could say? Which seems least like you? What do you make of these two answers?
4. One of the issues you will need to face in the final chapter, when we pull all of the puzzle pieces together, is what sex means. One place to start answering that question is by deciding whether you think the meaning of sex is given to us by God or is determined by us. Are there things in this chapter that incline you in one way or the other on this issue?
5. If you do not believe in God, what do the central values around which you organize your life tell you about how you want to live, sexually speaking?

Chapter 8

Why Do You Want to Have Sex?

*Y*ou have explored a number of issues at this point, including what kind of relationship you want to be in when you have sex, how you intend to treat other people, to what extent your consent is informed, whether you have made promises that influence your decision about having sex, the relevance of pregnancy and birth control to your situation, the importance of protection against STIs, and your primary values and religious beliefs. In this chapter, we are going to explore your reasons for wanting to have sex. This is your eighth puzzle piece. Were you to have sex now, what reasons would you give for doing so? To show your love? For fun? To get over a broken heart? What is motivating you? Part of making good decisions, sexual or otherwise, is discovering our reasons for wanting to act in one way rather than another and assessing whether those reasons are good ones.

I invite you to use a very simple assessment tool here to help you ponder possible reasons for having sex. If you draw a straight horizontal line, with a zero (representing the worst reasons) at one end and a ten (representing the best reasons) at the other, and you place the various possible reasons for having sex on the line, you will soon have a visual depiction of your preferred reasons. To make the continuum as specific to you as possible, you can add in any reasons that are yours but are not mentioned here. By the end of the chapter, you can look at what you consider to be the best reasons for having sex and compare them to your current situation to see whether any of them apply. That won't make any decisions for you, of course, but it might help you in your discernment process.

This chapter will be a bit different from the previous ones, in that you won't find here much extended discussion of ideas. Instead, because there are so many possible reasons for wanting to have sex, we are simply going to name and explore nine of them:

- I want to take the next step in my relationship.
- I want to give a gift to my partner.
- I want to have fun and feel good.
- I want a relationship.
- I want to please my partner.
- I want to fit in.
- I want to get rid of my virginity.
- I want to live life my way.
- I want my power back.

"I Want to Take the Next Step in My Relationship"

It might feel to you as though this is the right time in your relationship to have sex. Consider this slightly idealized scenario: You and your partner have been together for three years now. You've experienced the usual ups and downs that are part of every relationship, but on the whole everything has been wonderful. The intellectual dimension of your relationship is strong: you are interested in one another's interests; you talk about your careers and goals together; you even discuss the news of the day regularly. The emotional dimension of your life is strong: you do your best to offer support and comfort in the hard times; you are in love with your partner; and there is just something about this relationship that feels right in your heart. The spiritual dimension of your relationship is also strong: the values around which you want to structure your lives are strikingly similar; your views on God are compatible; and you both believe that service to a needy world is essential to the good life. Finally, the physical dimension of your life is strong: you enjoy similar food and value exercise, running together a couple of times each week. Sexually, you have shared about everything except intercourse; as all of the other dimensions of your life continue to grow and strengthen, you have a sense that the time is right to take that step. The entire relationship is falling into place perfectly, and you're beginning to feel as though you are holding back on sex for no good reason.

Where would you place this reason on your continuum? Would it be a three because you think the next step in this relationship should be marriage? Would it be a nine because you think that sexual union is an appropriate way to celebrate that all the pieces of a relationship have come together? If you are thinking that this reason is yours, but your relationship is different than the one described, what is your sense of the kind of relationship in which sex is appropriate, and why? If you need help pondering this, you might take another look at chapter 3.

"I Want to Give a Gift to My Partner"

There are times when we simply love our partners and want to express that love by sharing ourselves fully. Here is the way one person recently put it in an e-mail to me.

> I think the main reason that I do it is because it's something special that I want to share with someone that I really care about and trust with my whole being. . . . We really did talk about having sex for a long time, and for a long time I wasn't ready to make that commitment to him. But after spending almost a year with him and seeing the type of person he is and how he cares about me, I decided that I was mature enough to handle something like this, and that it was definitely something that I wanted to experience with him. . . . I love my boyfriend; I tell him this every day. I think the most special way that I can show that I love him is through giving him the gift of all that I am, and if I were to die tomorrow, I would want him to know that.

What do you think? On your continuum, is this a one or a ten or somewhere in between? Perhaps pondering the nature of gifts will help clarify the issue. True gifts are given expecting nothing in return. Of course, even if we expect nothing, it feels good to see our gifts received well. Some responses can bring us real joy, such as when someone accepts our gift in the spirit we intend it, when the person's reaction is joy and happiness, and when the gift binds us more deeply together. Some responses, on the other hand, can be hurtful, such as when someone laughs at a gift that is not intended to be funny, or when someone rejects an offered gift, throwing it back in our faces. At least some of these responses have analogies when the gift is sexual. To what extent does the possible result of giving your gift influence your desire to give it?

The woman writing above talks about giving "the gift of all that I am." Does it make a difference how much of oneself one wants to give in sex? Depending on our past experiences, we might be rather tentative about having sex. We might hold back a bit of who we are emotionally, for instance, because we were badly hurt the last time we gave our all to someone. Is wanting to give all that we are a better reason to have sex than wanting to give *most* of who we are? Would you put these in different places on the continuum?

By the way, before we leave this possible reason for having sex, you might add to your list of reasons something else this woman suggests, namely, that she wants to *express her love* for her boyfriend by giving herself as a gift. Expressing love for someone is frequently given as a reason for having sex, though we have not listed it independently here. Where would you place expressing love on your continuum? Is it a good reason? If so, how good? Where would you place expressing *like*?

"I Want to Have Fun and Feel Good"

"Sometimes you just want to get laid," I once heard a young woman say. Not everyone would put it that way, but many of us might be sympathetic to the feeling. Sometimes, especially once we have had sexual intercourse, nothing else will quite work: We don't want oral sex; we don't want to masturbate or have someone else masturbate us. These things are fun and feel good, but they are not the same as being inside someone or having someone inside you. The union, intimacy, and orgasms of sexual intercourse can feel great (acknowledging that most women and some men do not regularly orgasm through vaginal intercourse alone, but may need other, simultaneous stimulation). And sometimes, we just want one or more of these.

Consider a slightly different example. I was teaching a young-adult Sunday school class on moral issues. The topic of the week was sex. Afterwards, I was walking out of the church building with one of the participants who said, "I think of sex as adult play." With the advent of the pill and our knowledge that the use of condoms can lessen the spread of STIs, some of the risk, and especially the appearance of risk, has gone out of having sex. This may have the effect of making sexual encounters easier to contemplate and more relaxing to have. Since most of us love to touch and be touched, and since the physical pleasure attached to sex can be positively overwhelming, we are quite reasonably attracted to the fun of having sex.

Under what conditions would you say that feeling great and having fun are good reasons for having sex? Are there times when these motivations might rank as tens on your scale and times when they might rank as ones? Would it matter what kind of relationship you are in? What reasons on the part of your partner would match your desire to have fun or pleasure? What motivations on his or her part would make for problems with expressing your fun-seeking motivations?

"I Want a Relationship"

There are moments and places when we long for a relationship. I have felt this at a number of lonely times in my life. People in small colleges are among those who understand how lonely it can be when everyone around us is coupled up, and we are not. People in urban settings have impressed on me the sense of urgency that can sometimes come over us when we run into someone who actually might be interested in us, instead of being only interested in the casual relationships of urban life. The apparent popularity of dating or relationship-finding sites such as match.com and eHarmony.com suggests that finding meaningful relationships is difficult. Shows such as *The Bachelor, The Bachelorette, Dating in the Dark,* and *More to Love* are typically filled with refrains about the difficulty of establishing lasting relationships.

The feeling of urgency to find a relationship does not always end when we have one; sometimes it is replaced by a sense of urgency about keeping the relationship. We do not want to move backwards (as we often think of it) to being alone, and we are sometimes inclined to do just about anything we can to keep our coupled status. What can we do? Can we send flowers? Can we back up to the point where things started to go wrong and do things over? Can we reason our partner back into relationship with us? Can we change somehow, to make her or him love us? Suppose we could look better, or wear nicer clothes, or give more compliments, or buy better presents, or start paying more attention in conversations; would these things work?

It is not unusual for sex to be added to the list of the things we are willing to do for a relationship. We often think sex will give the person what he or she wants and show our dedication to the relationship. We are pretty sure if we don't have sex, the other person will leave us. As one colleague wrote to me about the attitude of some friends: "Failure to have sex indicates a relationship that isn't going anywhere." And no one wants to be in a relationship that is going nowhere. Maybe you can hold on to your partner if you give him or her sex, or maybe not, but if you really want to have someone, the chance feels worth it.

Good reason? Bad reason? What do you think? Where would you add "wanting a relationship" or "wanting to keep a relationship" on your continuum? Is it a better reason than having fun? Is it a worse reason than expressing love? If you are keeping your continuum in front of you, either mentally or on paper, you should slowly be developing a sense of what you consider good and bad reasons. You should be starting to get a sense of what is important to you when it comes to having sex.

"I Want to Please Him/Her"

The motivation to please someone can take at least two forms. It might revert back to the previous motivation, where you want to please your partner in order to keep him or her around. That is not the way I intend it here, though. I have in mind the kind of situation in which your partner wants sex (either now or always), but you are not interested *at the moment*. You are tired, or you are busy, or you are simply not in the mood to be sexual, but your partner is. Your motivation, then, is to give your partner sexual attention for no other reason than because she or he wants it.

You can imagine your degree of motivation varying a good bit in these cases, in part depending on other features of your relationship. For instance, if you wake up in the morning after a one-night stand and find that your partner wants to have sex again, would you be more or less likely to go against your own desires to give her or him sex than you would if you were in a long-term and committed relationship, in which the two of you had a history of mutual giving in the area of sex as well as other aspects of your life together? You might, therefore, want to ponder this particular motivation in the light of the quality of your overall relationship.

Another important issue here is whether we are giving selflessly or without a self. This is not always an easy distinction to make. When we do not have a well-formed, independent self, we can end up being defined by others. Our wants and desires become the same as the wants and desires of another person, not out of our own choice but because we cannot discern our own wants and desires. We do not make our own choices; instead, we mold ourselves to the choices of another person. There is a lack of awareness and a lack of voluntariness about our behavior in such cases. Giving selflessly, on the other hand, is a matter of knowing who we are, having given definition to ourselves but choosing to put someone or something else first in the situation. We choose to give of our well-formed self for the good of another. In a relationship, we would hope for this to be a mutual giving, one that enables both partners to experience the depths of both giving and receiving. Obviously, giving selflessly and giving with no self are very different contexts for giving, though we can name a possible reason to want to have sex—I want to please my partner—in almost the same way in each case. How would you rate these two different kinds of desire to please on your continuum?

"I Want to Fit In"

To varying degrees, we all want to be accepted by others. Some of us are fortunate because we have found places to "fit in" along the way, so we are pretty sure we will be accepted in new situations, as well. Others of us are less lucky and go through life never quite feeling accepted and never having the sense we might feel differently one day. Whichever group we fall into, we can be influenced to have sex by pressure from our peers, either those we fit in with or those we do not fit in with: "If I give him the sex he obviously wants, then I will be included in things with him and his friends; if I don't, then they probably won't ever include me in anything." Or "She wants to have sex. If I don't have sex with her, everybody's going to find out, and I'll get all kinds of grief from my teammates." Where does "fitting in" belong on the continuum? If what it takes to fit in with the people around me is having sex, someone might ask, is that a price I am willing to pay?

The location of this reason on your continuum may tell you something not only about what you consider to be good reasons for having sex but also what you think sex means. We can imagine someone thinking, "I'm not a virgin. I've started seeing someone new, and that person wants to have sex. I like it when I can enter into the conversations about sex that are all around me. What's the big deal?" We can also imagine someone thinking, "Having sex just to get other people to feel a certain way about me would compromise my view of sex as special and my view of myself as special, regardless of what anyone else thinks." Each of these differences is related to the desire to fit in, which is why your continuum may well be unique to you: no one else's life matches yours exactly.

It seems to me that wanting to fit in derives from, or is at least closely related to, the desire or need to be loved. My sense from listening to people over the years is that this desire is a common reason or motivation for making out with someone and only a bit less common as a reason for having sex. It may overlap, blend with, or even generate reasons such as wanting to be cared about or taken care of, wanting to be held or touched, wanting to feel special, and wanting to fit in, but wanting to be loved seems to be the deepest and most powerful of these wants and reasons.

Some of us have grown up with a hole in our souls because we either were not loved or were not loved well in our early years. Sometimes we turn to constructive ways of trying to fill or heal these holes, and sometimes we turn to destructive approaches. Is reaching for sex to help us feel loved for a night or a lifetime a constructive or destructive approach to meeting our desire to be loved? Where does it fall on your continuum?

"I Want to Get Rid of My Virginity"

Books have been written about the history and meaning of virginity and what inspires people to "lose" it, and I am not going to repeat that material here. It is worth pondering for a moment, however, what we mean by virginity. Does having either vaginal or anal or oral sex make one no longer a virgin? Is it only vaginal sex and anal sex? Or, contrary to all of this, is virginity a state of innocence about sex, perhaps spiritual, emotional, or intellectual? If you lose your innocence about what sex looks like and feels like, have you in some meaningful sense lost your virginity?

I hope these questions lead you to think about the deeper issue of why we want to define virginity in the first place. Are we trying to make an anatomi-cal statement, a statement about what activity someone may or may not have engaged in, or a statement about some deeper aspect of someone's state of being or awareness? These kinds of issues are important to ponder for your-self if you are thinking of having sex in order to lose your virginity. What, exactly, do you want to lose, and how is the insertion of a penis into a vagina, for instance, going to do that?

This said, certainly there are stigmas involved here. There is a stigma attached to being a virgin in some circles, and there is a stigma attached to not being a virgin in other circles. I have known Christians who did not want to tell their close Christian friends that they had lost their virginity because of the high value put on virginity in some Christian circles. And I have known people who felt like they had really accomplished something when they first had sex and were treated differently, at least during an initial period of cele-bratory winking, by their friends. One of the reasons we may decide to have sex is that we want to get rid of our virginity, defined in a certain way by some certain group. Where does the desire not to be a virgin fit on your con-tinuum of good and bad reasons for having sex? Is this related to your own peer group? Can you step outside of that peer group and try to think about the issue without other people's influence? Would that change your assessment of this reason?

"I Want to Live My Life My Way"

For many of us, the decision-making process around having sex is filled with what we have been told by parents, churches, mentors, and any number of people and groups. *Be abstinent*, say our schools. *Get laid*, say our peers. *Sex is fun, and you should go to it*, says the television. *Only in marriage*, says the church. *Do it*, or *Don't do it*, or *Just be safe*, or *I don't want to talk about it*, say our parents. Many of these voices swirl through our heads when we think about having sex, and, in response, some of us just declare we are going to live our own way, dismiss all of the noise, and have sex.

Sometimes we are declaring our way of life, our own values, when we choose to have sex. We decide this is one area of life where we are going to define ourselves. We are growing up, we say, and we are carving out our own identity in the midst of all that has defined or would define us. We might see this as a positive choosing of values. On the other hand, we might be choosing negatively. We might be deciding our own values only *over against* someone else's. "My parents are very conservative, and I'm sick of living their way. My boyfriend and I are having sex, no matter what they think." This is, at least possibly, not so much an affirmation of who one is as it is an affirmation of who one is not: "I am not my parents. I might decide later to choose the same values as my parents, but, at the moment, I am going to do anything except what they would have me do."

Self-definition can certainly be a good thing; it is part of what enables us to become adults. On the other hand, self-definition can be a troubling thing, depending on the nature of the values we reject: Not too many of us would affirm that defining ourselves as car thieves is a great idea. Rebellion, too, can be a good thing. Sometimes we have to react against those who shape or would shape us in order to find the freedom to become our true selves. Rebellion, of course, also may not be so good, for us or for anyone else, if we rebel by harming other people. Think about what this means in your own situation: Do these ideas of self-definition and rebellion shed light on whether wanting to live your own way adds to the good reasons or the bad reasons on your continuum, or do you think some other reason is really behind wanting to live your own way?

"I Want My Power Back"

Forced sexual intercourse is never right, but it is widespread. As a tool of war, as a way of controlling women and others, as a horrid part of this broken world, rape is both widespread and wrong. It is also a feature of the lives of many.

Not long ago, I was talking with a woman who had been raped in college. The story itself doesn't need to be shared here, but if you know anything about rape, you know that the experience was awful and the consequences were pervasive. A few months after this experience, the woman explained to me, she chose to have sex with someone she was in no particular relationship with, at least partly as a way of regaining the power she felt had been taken from her. She used him (and, it should be noted, with no reluctance or apparent expectations on his part) to reclaim herself, in a way. How would you understand this as a motivation for having sex? If you have had power stolen from you because of rape, childhood sexual abuse, or some other horror, where would its restoration fit on your continuum? As you ponder this, it might be worth exploring whether there are other ways of gaining power through sex that might be categorized and added to the continuum. We will talk again about power-related issues in chapter 10.

In this chapter, we have looked briefly at nine different motivations or reasons that are sometimes given for having sex. You might take a moment here to articulate any other reasons you can think of that are often given as reasons for having sex, and then add them to your continuum.

Your continuum is a simple way for you to keep track of your assessment of some of the many reasons people give for having sex. Are they good reasons or bad reasons? If they are bad, how bad; if they are good, how good? You can also see the continuum as a visual depiction of some of your values, at least as they apply to sex. The reasons you placed lower on your list (toward the "zero" side of the continuum) are probably not the reasons that will move you to have sex, at least insofar as you act in accordance with your values. If, for instance, you marked "I want to fit in" as a two on the continuum, you either will not be having sex in order to fit in, or you will have sex in order to fit in but then, if you react like most people who act against their values, feel guilty about it and wish you had not done it.

The higher-numbered reasons (toward the "ten" side of the continuum) are among those that might well motivate you to have sex. If you marked "to give a gift" as a good reason to have sex, then, at least if you are really capturing yourself and your view of sex, you might well be motivated by that reason. That does not say it *will* be the reason you have sex, and it doesn't say you will give this gift anytime soon, but it does make clear that you see sex as something to be valued highly.

As you ponder the puzzle of whether you are going to have sex, knowing how you value a wide variety of reasons can help you see whether you are currently in a situation in which you could reasonably and rightly express your higher values and not your lower-rated ones. This kind of self-understanding is one of the important consequences of exploring this eighth puzzle piece.

Questions for Reflection and Discussion

1. With just two more puzzle pieces to go, this might be a good time to take stock of your thinking about whether to have sex. At the start of this eighth chapter, I listed the major topics we have explored so far. How have they been fitting together for you? What do you think your decision about having sex is at this time, and why?
2. We mentioned a couple of times in the chapter adding your own possible reasons for having sex to your continuum. If you haven't done that yet, you might take this opportunity to do it and to see what you learn about yourself in the process.
3. This book assumes that we should have good reasons for the things we do, especially when they are such morally charged things as sex. Do you agree or disagree? Why?
4. Among the people you know well enough to be able to discern their reasons for having sex or not having sex, what is the most common reason, in either direction? Where does that reason fit on your continuum? Are you like or unlike the people you know well on this issue?
5. We could have included in this chapter a set of reasons *not* to have sex and put those on a continuum as well. Taking only a minute or two to think about it, what would you say are your top five reasons not to have sex with someone? How are those relevant to your life today?

Chapter 9

Who Might Be Affected?

*I*t is easy to think of sex as a private matter. Most of the time, people having sex take steps to ensure that they are not seen, by closing or even locking doors and drawing curtains or blinds, and not heard, even to the extent of attempting to quiet their natural responses. In the end, unless one has an exhibitionist streak, few people, if any, will know any specifics about what one does sexually unless they are told. The world has limited or no access to what happens in that room "behind closed doors."

At the same time, having sex may well have effects, most of them unintended, on many people. It affects you and your partner, certainly. It affects anyone you tell about having sex. It affects any number of relationships, if all we mean by that word is the way things are between two people (your relationship with your partner, with your parents, with your friends, with your partner's family and friends, to use simple examples). It affects your future partners or spouse. It affects your relationship with God or church community. It may affect the common good. These effects can go largely unnoticed, and it is our task here to explore some of them. As you see which of these might apply to your situation, you will be better able to make a good decision about whether to have sex. In addition to those you have pondered in earlier chapters, what consequences can you see to having sex, and are those consequences you want to bring about? Answering that question will give you the shape of your ninth puzzle piece.

Your Partner Is Affected

As I have spoken with people in recent months, it has become clear that, at least for many of us, one of the major factors in deciding whether to have sex with someone is whether it will harm her or him in some way. Will it lead the person on, in effect telling the lie that we care in a way we don't or that we are looking for a kind of relationship that we are not? In the odd sexual environment we are all in, where having sex seems to be much easier than talking about it with a current or prospective partner, it is easy to have sex and wake up not knowing what, if anything, it meant to the person beside you. Consider this example:

> Ethan and Jen were graduate-school lovers who kept in touch after their relationship ended. One time, when Jen had just gone through a painful break-up, they met for dinner and ended up in bed together. Along the way, Jen was honest with Ethan: "You can't count on me for anything. Please don't spend the night with me if you are expecting anything. I'm not starting any kind of relationship now." Ethan heard her, but he loved her and loved having sex with her. A few weeks later, when Jen said she was not interested in an exclusive relationship, Ethan was hurt and felt angry and betrayed. He pulled back from his friendship with Jen, which hurt her, as she had been honest with him.

I spoke with Jen and Ethan shortly after these events. Jen felt hurt and betrayed because she had been honest with Ethan, and he had seemed to accept what she said but then deserted their friendship. Ethan felt hurt and betrayed because, though he could accept that he and Jen might not be a couple again, he couldn't understand why she would sleep with him but not want a relationship. He couldn't seem to fit together her needs with his feelings of connection with her during their night together.

Even our convictions that our attempts at communication have been successful and that we understand where things stand can prove illusory when having sex runs up against deep emotions, hopes, or dreams. What we do about this reality is our question. Jen and Ethan could have not had sex, which seems unlikely given that they had had sex before and shared a great love and passion for one another. They might have spent more time talking about how they felt, or they might have been more aware of where they stood. In the end, they both had to deal with feelings of hurt and betrayal. Granted, your prospective sexual relationship may not have all of these other dimensions attached to it, but how does knowing that you cannot predict all the effects of your encounter, even if your communication with your partner appears to be excellent, shape your decision to have sex or not to have sex?

You Are Affected

In addition to our partners, we too can be affected by having sex, sometimes positively and sometimes negatively. On the one hand, sex can be great fun.

Everything from the first thought of the possibility in our mind to the glow of the post-union cuddle and the knowing smiles in the days that follow can be sheer delight. Sex can bring great physical pleasure and deep emotional joy. Being touched, with our consent and eagerness, by someone who cares deeply about us can make us feel content in ways few other human activities can. In the vulnerability of two people sharing the most intimate of human physical connections, we can be carried out of ourselves to what some see as union with the other, the cosmos, and even God.

On the other hand, sex can also bring us agony. As one person wrote to me,

> I have, more often than I'd like to admit, given too much of myself to someone physically and experienced what my friends and I call a "soul hangover."

In the words of another,

> Do I care enough about this person, and does he care enough about me, to really give all of myself to him and to really receive all of him . . . or am I just feeling wild and frisky? When the second is the case, no matter how much fun I had doing it, I'll wake up the next day, and some sort of dull chasm has separated in my chest. . . .

Having sex can bring regret, guilt, and shame, and it can contribute to a low self-image. Its inescapable vulnerability, its power to influence our innermost dimensions even when we don't know it, can bring us surprising aches. I asked a friend in his fifties about this, and here are his words:

> Including my wife, I have had sex with seven people in my life. Some were friends; some I loved deeply or grew to love deeply. What surprises me now, as I look back, and when I have no contact with most of them except my wife, is that they all live in my heart in some way. It's not that I think about them every day or even every month, but they each carry a small piece of my heart, and each could, if they so desired, wound me today if they, in some way, rejected me or dismissed what we shared.

It seems unlikely to me that most people would describe their past lovers in these ways, but I include the quotation here for two reasons. First, it points to an effect on us that we may or may not be aware of when we have sex with someone, an effect that may occur whether or not we intend or desire it. Second, it might help to dispel the notion that only women are really emotionally or spiritually affected by having sex. That is a popular view, but even if we men act as though it is true sometimes, it is mostly nonsense.

As you ponder having sex, what can you do to make it more likely that sexual intercourse's effects will be those of pleasure and contentment and not pain and heartache? Not much is guaranteed in this world, of course, but we can certainly improve the odds of the future going in one direction rather than another, whether that future is tomorrow or decades from now. What do you want for yourself, tomorrow and years from now? How does that shape the sex you have or do not have today?

Your Relationship Is Affected

At the end of chapter 2 and throughout chapter 3, we noted the importance of thinking about relationships, not just the people who stand in them. After all, none of us can be described or understood fully unless our relationships are included in the process. We are brothers and sisters, children and parents, friends and lovers, and these things are essential to us in the sense that were particular ones of them to change, we would be different. Our relationships, frankly, take us from being no one to being someone in particular.

Given the significance of our relationships in our lives, one of the ways we should think about the effects of a decision to have sex is by focusing not just on the two people involved but on the relationship between them. How, for instance, might having sex affect not just the friend with whom I have it but the friendship itself? Might sex enhance our relationship and draw us closer in lasting ways? Might it take things in the other direction, ruining the closeness we have and making us more like strangers to one another? This is not the first time we have raised this question, but this is an appropriate place to remind ourselves of its importance.

Your Friends and Peers Are Affected

Wander back for a moment to our original thoughts on sex as private. To what extent is sex a private matter between partners, and to what extent are others potentially affected? Is what we do "our business," having no impact on the lives of others that makes any difference to us, or is our business essentially and necessarily the business of others? Here is a short list of some of the influences that one person or couple having sex might have on others.

- A friend decides to have sex or not based on what we have done.
- A peer or younger sibling learns to treat men or women in a certain way because that is the way we have modeled for them.

- Our new and close bond with one person changes our relationships with others.
- One friend celebrates our joy; another is jealous of it; a third is disappointed in us.
- Our experience with a new dimension of life changes our sense of self, which, in turn, has an impact on those around us.
- Our enhanced or injured self-image brings out concern in some people we know and avoidance from others.

Notice that some of these instances require that others know that we have had sex while other instances merely require that others come under the influence of the subtle changes in us that stem from our decision to have sex or not. Either way, what remains private (in that others have restricted access to it) is something about the moments two people were together, while what are not private are whatever effects having sex or not having it had on them. Although the decision to have sex or not have sex is a deeply *personal* one because of the many ways in which our decision can define us and make us vulnerable, it is seldom a *private* decision, given the extent to which it radiates outward in the kind of people we are and how we treat others.

God Is Affected

I once asked a group of people what reasons they could give me for abstaining from sex until marriage. A number of answers were given fairly quickly, after which there was a short pause. Looking around the room, one of the quieter members of the group then said quite intensely, "Well, I was waiting for someone else to say it, but how about because the Creator of the universe told us not to have sex until we're married and is angry and disappointed if we don't obey?" If you view God in any kind of personal and relational way, then you may well find it appropriate to ask whether God is affected by what you do sexually. After all, the biblical God is clearly affected by such things as obedience, disobedience, persistent prayer, and human needs, and the vast majority of Christians show their confidence in God's responsiveness through the widespread practice of intercessory prayer. The Christian God is not typically conceived as hopelessly distant from us but instead as affecting and being affected by daily human life.

To say God is or might be affected is not, obviously, to consider the *how* question. Since you have already been invited in chapter 7 to consider how you understand God, let's simply note here that the more personlike you consider God to be, the more you are likely to see God's reactions as covering the gamut of human emotions. If you take God to be very much like a person, then

God might be, for instance, angry, sad, delighted, amused, disappointed, joyful, outraged, or confused by our sexual behavior. If you take God to be very unlike a person and more like, say, a river of love carrying us along through time, space, and eternity, then the effect on God of our having sex or not having sex might be less immediate or emotional and more a slight enhancement of or impediment to the river's flow. The question would still be how God is affected by what we do, but the possible effects might be quite different.

Assuming you made progress on articulating your own view of God in chapter 7, what are the possible ways, emotional or otherwise, that your God might be affected by your moral decision about having sex? Does this guide your decision in any way?

The World Might Be Affected

Finally, does it make sense to go beyond what we have already pondered and wonder whether the world around us, in senses that are broader than anything we have discussed to this point, might be affected by our decisions about sex? We have seen ways that the people and relationships around us might be affected, and this means that the faith communities and other groups composed of these people and relationships would be affected. Without going so far as to suppose that everyone in the world or any particular person on the other side of the world would be affected by our particular sexual choices, there is a way that we might take one final and sweeping step in our attempt to discern the shape of this ninth puzzle piece. Let's consider whether our sexual decisions have any effect on the common good.

The common good is a concept often used by ethical, political, and theological thinkers, and it means essentially what it seems to mean: the good of all. Concern for the common good stands in for questions such as, What is in the best interests of the group, the community, the world, or the creation? Consider every moral decision we might make: whether to boycott a product, lie to a friend, cheat on an exam, risk one life to save another, defend ourselves against attack, or have sex. In each case, we might try to make our decision by considering the common good: How would cheating on an exam, for instance, affect the good of all? Would it enable the cheater to get a better grade and contribute more to the world? Would it contribute to a societal breakdown of trust? Might it do a bit of both?

We can apply the same approach to having sex. How would having sex or not having sex contribute to or detract from the good of all? Could there be a profound ripple effect in creation, such that seemingly small actions, including whom you sleep with tonight, might not only affect you and some small number of people around you but also, by introducing something right or wrong into the world, all of us? Could we be this interconnected? If so, how would this interconnection to the larger world shape a particular decision of whether or not to have sex?

Obviously, a complete investigation of this question would take infinite time and space, but the following story illustrates what I have in mind:

> Josh and Beth are friends who have consensual and enjoyable sex in their senior year of college. After graduation, they go their separate ways. Josh heads to Florida, where he enrolls in graduate school to become a social worker; Beth heads to California and tries her hand at becoming a writer. Josh's friend, Rory, who knew both Josh and Beth in college and had a crush on Beth, finds out a year after graduation that Josh and Beth slept together. Josh, not wanting to hurt Rory's feelings, had lied to Rory about this, so Rory is currently not speaking to Josh. Rory's wife, Pam, finds Rory to be rather possessive sometimes, and one day understands that it is because he felt betrayed by Josh and doesn't want anyone to come between him and Pam. Pam and Rory eventually divorce because of Rory's possessiveness. Pam has primary custody of their daughter, Eve, who often hears from her mother the importance of being sure prospective boyfriends don't seem controlling in any way. Meanwhile, Josh, who has become a social worker, is able to assure his clients that sex is not always violent and abusive but can sometimes be a fun, friendly behavior that leaves one with good feelings for years. Beth has, by this time, published her first novel, which draws on her sexual experiences with Josh to depict how friends can become sexual with one another without destroying their friendship. Josh reads Beth's book and understands how she was influenced by their time together. One of the things that keeps him going is his awareness, shaped by what Beth wrote, that things we do not think will mean much can, in the long run, mean a lot.

Am I taking this too far? Yes and no. Yes, because it is not just the sexual experience Josh and Beth had that shaped all of these occurrences around the world. But no, because it is *partly* their sexual experiences that shaped these occurrences, and in ways they could not ever have imagined. Somehow or other, what we do affects the world. Little by little, that effect spreads. Perhaps its effects are less powerful the farther in time and space from the original event we get, or perhaps its effects are strengthened by other events along the way. We don't know, and we can't know.

If we can't know, should we care? You will have to make a judgment here as you continue your discernment process, but it seems to me that the uncertainty of the impact, positive or negative or both, of what we do makes our decisions not less important but more important. If we cannot know what the impact of our decisions will be, then having them be the right ones, according to our very best judgment at the time, becomes a necessity. Will we always decide rightly? No. But there is much to be said for always giving it our best shot.

Final Thought

It is easy, it seems to me, to consider many of the decisions we make in life, including sexual ones, to be private, believing that others not only do not observe them but also are not affected by them. I am trying to suggest in this chapter that this approach to the way we think about our lives can be deceptive. Even though we often do not notice the impact of our sexual decisions, and even though we often seek to minimize that impact by not talking about them with many people, it is still reasonable to suppose that they are influential decisions in a number of ways. If nothing else, the decision to have sex or not can change us, and this, in turn, will have some impact on others with whom we have contact.

Obviously, we have here another multisided puzzle piece. How does it fit into your puzzle? Soon, we will look at four possible ways to pull all the puzzle pieces together to form coherent answers to the question of whether or not to have sex. Before we do that, however, let's look at a few final questions on piece nine and then turn to piece ten: the role of power in your sexual encounter or relationship.

Questions for Reflection and Discussion

1. Other than you and your partner, can you name two people who would somehow be affected by your choice to have or not have sex? How would they be affected? Does this contribute in any way to your thinking about whether or not to have sex?
2. One of this chapter's difficult issues is whether God is influenced by our moral decisions. If you believe in God, how would you answer the question and why? If you do not believe in God, what do you think is the best way for those who do believe to think about this question?
3. Ponder this very moving scenario from the point of view of the questions in this chapter:

I wondered if there would ever be a time when I would think that I should have waited until marriage. . . . I have always thought the phrase "making love" was very extreme, but that night I truly feel like we did make love. . . . I felt as though we had left our bodies behind and our souls were making love. It was wonderful and heartbreaking at the same time; it was almost as though we knew then that in the long run our lives would venture down different paths. However, the question I had been asking myself over and over, "Was it worth the pain?" was answered that night. It was worth every second of it. I had loved completely and in return had been completely loved; who could ask for anything better?

Chapter 10

What Kind of Power?

*P*ower is simply the ability to do something or to bring about change in a condition or situation. We all have power of some kind or other and to some extent or other, and power is a component of all human relationships, where it may be used either for good or for evil. Our tenth and final puzzle piece is awareness of where power might lie in the interaction between you and another person, so that you can more freely choose whether having sex is a good idea.

This chapter is in three parts. In the first part, we will look at issues related to power generally, including what it is, the differences between potential and actual power, and the exercise of power by individuals and groups. In the second part, we'll explore the coercive use of power, both in relationships between professionals and their clients and in rape. In line with the second chapter's minimum moral standard of not harming others, we will assume here that you are not planning to use power coercively but that you want to understand some of the situations in which coercive power is used and especially those in which coercive power might be directed toward you. The latter are presumably situations you wish to avoid. In the third and final section, we'll talk about using power to build relationships instead of harming them. As we begin reflecting on power generally, you might ponder whether you see power being used constructively or destructively between you and anyone with whom you might be thinking about having sex.

A Basic Look at Power

We show that we have the power to do something simply by doing it, and everything we do is a demonstration of our power. Consider four examples:

- We send a text message.

- We drive to our favorite coffee shop.
- We buy the newest version of the Kindle e-book reader.
- We cheer on a friend who is running a marathon.

As with all of our actions, we can ask of each of these instances whether it is morally positive, negative, or neutral. If we don't supply any additional context for the above list, most of us would probably consider the first three to be morally neutral actions and the fourth to be a morally positive example of kindness. On the other hand, someone might protest that wasting gas to get coffee that I could easily make at home is not very eco-friendly or cost effective, and someone else might claim that buying e-book readers actually harms the publishing industry and wastes money on toys while people around the world are starving. Such concerns could turn our evaluations from neutral to negative. The point with looking at these simple cases, however, is to recognize that asking moral questions about exercises of power is a normal part of daily life and critical reflection.

Sometimes, of course, we do not need to think globally to find moral problems with simple acts; sometimes power is used in ways that our common moral sense tells us immediately are right or wrong. Consider these examples:

- We spend a day working on a Habitat for Humanity construction project, or we give blood to the Red Cross.
- We help a friend find a job.
- We write test answers on our forearm and cheat on a test.
- We steal ten dollars from our roommate's wallet.

Clearly, we would tend to consider the first two uses of power right or good and the second two wrong or bad, at least under most circumstances we can imagine. In the first two, we are exercising our power in ways that are helpful to others, and in the third and fourth cases, we are using power immorally, something we signaled by using the words "cheat" and "steal" in our descriptions.

With equal ease, and to make similar points, we can also generate a list of examples of using power in the sexual realm, though perhaps we will find less initial agreement on their moral evaluation. Consider these, for instance:

- We give someone an erotic massage.
- We French-kiss a friend.
- We invite our sexual partner to try a new sexual position.
- We masturbate, alone.

My guess is that most of us immediately want more details before morally evaluating most of these, in part because many expressions of sexual power carry with them significant social baggage but also because we realize that such expressions often entail great human vulnerability. So we want to know who is giving whom an erotic massage and whether the giver and receiver have the same intentions. We want to know what kind of friend is being kissed and whether consent is present. Some of us will get queasy at the idea of sexual positions, while others may think such experimentation is fun but want to know more about the relationship and the setting. And some of us probably think masturbation is immoral, regardless of the circumstances, while others of us are just sad that we have to do it alone.

In addition to being able to think of our lives in terms of using power and being able to explore whether its use has morally positive or morally negative components, a few distinctions and definitions will come in handy as we explore using power sexually. The first one is the distinction between *actual* and *potential* uses of power. The actual use of power is obvious: all of the examples above are instances of power actually being used, whether to buy a Kindle, steal money, or kiss a friend. Potential uses of power, on the other hand, are situations in which someone has the ability to do something but does not do it. In most cases, any two people sitting on a sofa have the power to kiss one another, but the vast majority of the time they do not use that power. Their power is only potential.

We will note in the following section why this distinction is important, but here it is worth noting that merely having the power to do something, as a matter of potential power, does not mean we would be right to do it. We all have the ability to do many things that we do not do because we believe we should not. We probably could kiss that person sitting next to us on the sofa, for instance, even though we know that she or he would not consent if asked. Indeed, we could do any number of acts of theft, lying, cheating, and other mayhem, but we choose not to, because we know they would be wrong. Much of our power for destruction goes unused, which is surely a good thing.

The second distinction we should make is between individual and group power. Individuals exercise power, and groups exercise power. To get a few examples of the latter in our minds now, consider these: A construction crew builds a house. A family goes Christmas caroling. A basketball team plays a game. A society enforces its laws. Each example happens only because of the individual exercises of power by the group's members, but much more is accomplished by the group than any of the individuals alone could do. Indeed, the relationships built among the members of each group generate power that the mere collection of team members could not match. We will talk more about group power in the two following sections, the first on power used coercively and the second on power used mutually.

Using Power Coercively

To use power coercively is to override other people's consent or free choice to get them to act or to act on them in ways they would not otherwise choose. Since the instances we are going to discuss are going to be negative, it is worth noting that there are uses of coercive power that some people find to be positive. If we are mugged on the street, many of us think knocking the mugger to the ground, a coercive move, would be justified. Certainly wars are filled with coercion that many who are fighting believe to be right. Also, consider grabbing someone about to commit suicide and preventing him or her from doing so, perhaps because we want to give that person time to reconsider. Of course, in this last case, we may think that we are overriding the person's current wishes because those wishes are not in accord with his or her *true* wishes, in which case the general rule against coercion might not apply because the person might not be competent to make her or his own decisions. But you see the point: there may be instances in which power used coercively is rightly used, even though those cases are not the ones with which we will be concerned. As a matter of fact, there may well be no instance where the coercive use of sexual power can be justified.

To begin our discussion of coercive uses of sexual power (the ability to act sexually), let's imagine two single people, Aidan and Mary. Setting aside for this discussion your view of whether single people should have sex, how would you evaluate the following situations with respect to coercive power?

- Aidan and Mary go to dinner. He pays, and she sleeps with him.
- Aidan and Mary sleep together; Mary gives Aidan an A in her class.
- Mary tells Aidan she loves him, and he sleeps with her.
- Aidan cheats at strip poker; when Mary is naked, Aidan seduces her.

What follows is one way to assess these situations; where does it differ from what you said? In the first example, we need to know whether Mary sleeps with Aidan because of some hold he has over her on account of paying for dinner. If Aidan is attempting to use his money to influence Mary to do something she would not otherwise do, and if Mary succumbs to this (perhaps without even noticing what is happening), we might well say that Aidan has misused his power. On the other hand, we could simply have a description of an evening that includes two people having both fully consensual dinner and fully consensual sex.

We can analyze the third case in much the same way as the first. Is Aidan doing something he doesn't really want to do or would not do because Mary, who doesn't really care about Aidan but wants sex and knows he feels unloved, uses his need against him to get what she wants? If so, this looks like a negative use of coercive power. But it could be nothing more than two people who love one another having sex.

The fourth example is a bit more complicated, as there are at least two places where power comes into play. If Aidan cheats at strip poker because he really wants to get Mary naked, and if she, for instance, only takes her clothes off because she is afraid Aidan will leave her if she doesn't go along with him, then we could easily make a case for a negative use of coercive power here. The second place coercive power might occur concerns the seduction, which may or may not be problematic. If Aidan and Mary are in a relationship and have had sex before, and if Aidan is successful at lovingly getting Mary "in the mood" when she isn't, we would probably evaluate that differently than the situation in which Mary is a touch-starved person whom Aidan knows does not want to sleep with him but whom he is pretty sure he can convince, regardless of what she wants.

The second case, in which Mary gives Aidan an A in her class at some point after they sleep together, raises issues all its own. It is generally thought that teachers having sex with their students, clergy having sex with parishioners, physicians having sex with their patients, counselors having sex with clients, and employers having sex with employees are abuses (morally bad uses) of power. Whatever other dimensions of power might be present in the relationship between Aidan and Mary, the power imbalance caused by the professional relationship is such that most people assume the free choice of the client is compromised. Could that analysis be reversed in specific circumstances? Certainly. Could it be that Aidan uses his very charismatic nature to get Mary into bed and that she gives him an A because he earns it? Sure. Could it be that there is no abuse of power in this situation? Yes, it could be so. Most professional organizations, however, recognizing the kind of professional power their members or practitioners hold, prohibit in advance any sexual relationships between professionals and those they serve.

In these situations, our distinction between actual and potential power becomes relevant, though it may raise as many issues as it solves. The typical prohibition of relationships such as those just mentioned, between a student and his or her teacher, for instance, might be supported in at least two ways. The first is that when sex occurs in these situations, it often does great harm, so it's important to build a wall that makes such potential harm impossible, even if there are cases where the relationship works out well. The second way of understanding these prohibitions is that there is a *mystique* of power that coerces or manipulates without the intention of the professional or the awareness of the client. This mystique of power is a feature of potential power that is worth keeping in mind. It is easy to feel, however unconsciously, that particular people have the power to heal or nurture us, even though they do not, and to respond to them sexually.

This quick look at the mystique of power reminds us that coercive power is often unconscious on the part of the individual, being built into ways we interact with one another in our social settings. Here's a reflection on this from a twenty-something:

> I think the most important thing (in considering whether to have sex), from a woman's standpoint at least, is whether they're having sex just to please the other person. There can be so much manipulation, guilt, pressure, insecurity, and power struggle tied up in those situations. I can't think of much that's less healthy and more degrading.

This is not a high recommendation for the current state of affairs. Terms such as "manipulation," "pressure," "power struggle," and "degrading," along with the idea of having sex just to please another person, suggest the kind of misuse of power that is typical of a climate where attempts abound to use power coercively.

This recognition of power *struggle* is important. To this point, we have mostly considered power being exerted in one direction, and there is no doubt but that often this is the way it feels and is. But the power being exerted in one direction can be met with a defensive power in the opposite direction, so that one person pushes for sex and the other person pushes back against having sex. Whether or not either kind of power is exerted consciously, the result of any use of coercive power and of any battle between aggressive and defensive power is that there are winners and losers: some people get what they want and some don't. Pause and think for a moment about the impact of this frequent feature of sexual relationships when it is extended from two competing individuals through the wider society.

The most told but not often-enough heard story in the use of coercive power is of men over women. Sexual coercion is, more often than not, learned and deeply embedded behavior that men exert, consciously or unconsciously, over women. This does not mean that women are not sexual *initiators* in relationships, but initiation and coercion are very different things. It seems to me that we are much more likely to hear a comment or observe an attitude such as this one from a man rather than a woman: "I'll stop nagging, manipulating, trying to make you feel guilty, arguing to convince you, threatening to end the relationship, looking at other people to make you feel insecure about us, pressuring you whenever we're alone, and all you have to do is have sex with me." Of course, modes of manipulation can differ, and one female reader mentioned women friends who say *withholding sex* from their male partners is a way they can exert power. Certainly, withholding may at times be a playful exercise ("No sex for you until I get my back rub," said with a wink), but if used manipulatively, withholding sex would also appear to be an exercise of coercive power.

Again, much of this is so deeply embedded in our ways of thinking and living that we are unconscious of it and can be quite shocked to see ourselves acting with even mild coercion. As awareness is the first step toward change, however, the shock can be a good step for us. Does thinking about coercive power help you to sort out any issues in your own life and relationships? Do you find yourself trying to overrule or overpower the free choices of your partner? Do you feel as though your own free choice is being eroded? Can you find a healthy way to rebalance the exercises of power so that each of you fully respects the choices of your partner?

As a last look in this section at the social side of our analyses, consider this comment and these questions on group coercive power.

> Readily available birth control has enormously increased women's sexual power in lots of situations, but has that power been subverted by an expectation to have sex because it comes with fewer material consequences? Has women's new sexual power been sort of kidnapped by male desire, or should we understand women to also desire these more casual sexual encounters? And how do you have equality in sexual relationships if you have asymmetry in social power?

Power Used Coercively: Rape

Laurie, a woman in her thirties, agreed to write for this book the final scenario about power being used coercively. I have put it in a separate section to highlight the importance of talking about and eliminating this horrific form of sexual coercion.

> Several years ago, I ran into an old friend from college at a party. We ended up talking and dancing for most of the evening. Over the next few weeks, we spent a lot of time together, first in groups and then by ourselves. I became comfortable with him and trusted his friendship. He said he was interested in me, but I told him I wasn't looking for a serious relationship with anyone. We often talked about our lives and our hopes for the future, and I mentioned to him at one point that I planned to keep my virginity until I was married. After one evening of conversation and drinks, we messed around some, but he knew I was not okay with having sex, and that seemed fine with him.

Weeks later, we went out with some friends. He kept buying me shots, and I ended up drinking way more than I ever do. Our friends took us to their house for the night, where I quickly headed to the guest room and went to bed. He came into my room shortly after that, but I still trusted him and didn't mind him sleeping next to me, and I fell back to sleep. I woke up sometime later, and he was pressed up against me and clearly wanted to have sex. I told him no and told him again that I did not do that and was not going to do that. I went back to sleep. I woke up later, and he was on top of me, having sex with me. It was as though a switch had been flipped: he was saying demeaning things and acting in ways that terrified me. It was horrible. Then, later, he started acting again like the friend I had thought he was. Now, years later, I think what he was after the entire time I knew him was my virginity. The day after it happened, I went and got the morning after pill and prayed for my period every day until it started. I haven't spoken with him or seen him since.

It has been a long time since that night, and I still have a problem trusting guys. I am more determined than ever to wait for the right person before I choose to have sex with anyone, and it will be on my terms the next time. I know some people feel as though once you've had sex, you might as well keep on having it, but I don't feel that way at all. I feel like because someone used his power against me, I have to be a much stronger person and wait until the time is right and the situation and conditions are on my terms.

A defining feature of the use of coercive power is that it "overpowers" others by overriding their freedom to choose their own path. It ignores and acts contrary to the consent of those who are acted upon. Rape is an extreme form of such abuse. In this situation, Laurie's expressed intention to wait to have sex until she was married was overridden. Her middle-of-the-night statement that she would not consent to sex was ignored. She was, quite possibly, too much under the influence of alcohol to give consent even if she had wanted to, which is the third grounds for calling what happened to her a rape. And though it may not be a legal dimension of rape, her trust in her "friend" was betrayed. This was, to use her word, a "horrible" instance of the use of coercive power.

The use of coercive sexual power, typically though not exclusively against women, has an undeniably social dimension. Think of the social climate described by the two reflections prior to Laurie's. Think of the mystique we attach to virginity and "deflowering a virgin." Think of the emphasis on our "first times" of having sex as some kind of rite of passage. Consider the ways we bombard people with the dual messages that virginity is bad and virginity is good. Also, think of the many ways we support aggression instead of peacefulness or gentleness in this society. These are just a few of the many contributing factors to a social setting in which unconscious uses of coercive sexual power abound.

We have covered a lot of difficult material to this point in our chapter, and it's worth pausing for a moment to reflect on it. Here's a question: Based on what you have just read and looking around at your own world, where do you see power being used in ways that contribute to healthy relationships and sexual encounters, and where do you see power being used in ways that contribute to unhealthy relationships and sexual encounters? More particularly, this final puzzle piece concerns how power is used in the relationship in which you are considering having sex. If you are trying to decide whether to have sex with your lover of three years, what does reflecting on power contribute to your thinking? If you are trying to decide whether it is appropriate to hook up on Friday night, how does the balance of power between you and the person you are likely to hook up with affect your decision? Do any of our reflections on social context and group coercive power influence your thinking at all? To conclude this section of our chapter and introduce the next one, here are a few situations you might ponder. Where is power present, and how might it be negotiated in these situations?

- Mary insists that Aidan use a condom, but he doesn't want to.
- Aidan and Mary watch a pornographic movie while having sex, in order to discover some different positions to try.
- Aidan insists that he and Mary drink more than usual before making out this time; Mary isn't sure about his intentions.
- Aidan wants Mary to have an HIV test before they have sex for the first time; Mary argues that because she has always used a condom in the past, the risk of transmission to him is negligible.

Develop different permutations of these basic situations until you are pretty sure you have figured out how to spot the exercise of coercive power or attempts to use it. Whoever you are, and whatever you choose to do sexually, this kind of reflection should serve you well as you make your way through the coercive sexual climate in which we live.

Power Used Mutually

We have looked at basic issues related to power, and we have explored the coercive use of power to try to override the freedom of others, ignore consent, and get one's own way. In this section, then, we want to look at a power that respects or even enhances the freedom of others, seeks not only consent but also well-being, and works cooperatively with the other person to set a mutual path. This is the end toward which the chapter and in some ways the entire book are moving: two people setting shared goals for their sexual sharing and pursuing those goals together. Let's start with an example that shows what we mean and then create a second example that we can try to understand together. Here's an example of two people, Erik and Stephanie, coming together to make a decision jointly that is, in the end, good for both of them.

> When I was a teenager, I didn't care much about religious teachings on sexuality. I professed Christianity's core beliefs, but I did not bother with applying these beliefs to my life. So when I thought I was ready, I started having sex with a boyfriend (who is now my husband).
>
> As I grew up, I decided to do more than just listen to sermons or go to church events. I began to study the Bible for myself. It was during this time of personal study that the Holy Spirit convicted me to stop having sex outside of marriage. I remember the exact moment. I realized that my sexual practice is completely related to the core of my faith. It was part of my daily struggle—the battle between the Spirit and the flesh (Romans 7–8). I recognized that my actions matter and that God cares about what I do. And sex as an unmarried woman was not in God's plan for me.
>
> So, I spoke with my (then) fiancé. He was supportive and understood my perspective. But he thought that once we started having sex, there wasn't any benefit in stopping. I thought there was benefit; every time we sin, Christ is crucified anew (Hebrews 6:6). We talked for a while and decided together not to have sex again until we were married. We kept our commitment and did not have sex for a year's time. Now after more than a year of marriage, I am so glad we made that commitment to doing our relationship right. I am a stronger person, and our marriage is better because of it!

Note how power might have been used differently in this situation. Stephanie might have declared that she was not having sex, regardless of what Erik thought, instead of actually engaging in a conversation. Erik might have responded by telling her that the relationship was over if she wouldn't have sex with him. Or he might have agreed but then tried to manipulate, cajole, plead, beg, guilt, or otherwise coerce Stephanie into having sex. One thing prevented these results, however: commitment to shared ends.

So many of the stresses that we face in our sexual lives are the result of not paying attention to shared ends. This can be true even if no attempts to coerce are present. We may not be caught in a bartering situation or in attempts to manipulate or otherwise get our way, but even respect for another person can be accompanied by hard feelings. If Erik said to Stephanie, "Well, I disagree, but I respect you and your right to make this decision," and the couple left things this way, even respect could turn into annoyance and relational stress. What can solve this is true, shared power: where the two are committed to an end beyond their own wills and choices and have turned their abilities to that common end. Stephanie and Erik analyzed their relationship and what was good for it, exploring how sexual expression connected with the religious faith to which they were both committed. Such faith is not necessary for the exercise of true mutual sexual power, but clear and honest communication surely is.

We do not want to wax too idealistic here, because it is clear that perfect mutuality and equality are unlikely in the real world, and Stephanie and Erik will certainly face challenges in the future. But when two or more people turn their power away from their individual aspirations and focus on mutual goals, some of the threat of coercive power dissipates and the possibility of power that empowers increases. Let's imagine a scenario and see whether we can articulate what it means to move from a focus on individual power assertion to power that is mutually concerned with a couple's well-being.

Isaac and Maria have hit a roadblock in their relationship. They have been seeing each other for about a year. They have not yet had sex, though they have mutual oral sex occasionally. Maria cannot see any reason why they should not go ahead and have intercourse. Isaac says he is not ready, especially since, before meeting Maria, he had intended not to do anything sexual until he got married. Maria has tried everything she can think of: dressing the way Isaac likes, cooking dinner for him as often as possible, giving him space to hang out with his friends when he wants to, asking him for sex when he is sexually stimulated, bringing a bottle of wine for them to drink on nights she knows she will be staying with him, and watching his favorite sporting events. She is getting tired of not getting what she wants and finds herself getting angry when Isaac won't let her do what she wants to in bed; for his part, Isaac is getting tired of Maria's persistence and is starting to be suspicious of her niceness.

If you were Isaac and Maria and thought there were enough good things about your relationship to make it worth working on, and you wanted to move your relationship from coercive power to mutual power, how would you do it? Is it possible in this situation? Let's end this chapter with a few thoughts on how these two might move beyond their impasse.

Mutual power only happens where there are shared goals, even if those shared goals are simply mutual pleasure. Without shared goals and a common understanding of the relationship, there can't be mutuality or equality of power. In the current case, it looks as though Maria is intent on one thing: sex with Isaac. She is doing a number of good things, but their goodness is diminished if not eliminated by the intention behind them. Isaac seems to be feeling a bit guilty about his current sexual behavior, which makes him even more reluctant to go further. And, of course, there is nothing like suspicion of someone else's motives to get rid of any romantic urges. So the first thing Maria and Isaac need to do is to take some time for introspection and see if they really want this relationship. Does Maria care about Isaac and want to continue growing with him, or is she only interested in him if he will sleep with her? Does Isaac see in Maria someone he wants to continue to grow with and care about, or are his feelings for her too damaged at this point?

Let's assume Isaac and Maria have both decided they want to continue the relationship. They care enough about each other and value the time they have spent and memories they have made together too much to give up now. The next step, unless it has already been done as a component of the first, is to figure out where they individually stand on sex. Isaac needs to come to terms with what his feelings of guilt are telling him and how he wants to be living his life.

Once these things have been sorted out individually, Isaac and Maria need to have a deeply honest conversation or series of conversations, expressing how they feel and what their bottom lines are. This is part of the process of coming together on the meaning, direction, and goals of the relationship. Power exercised mutually orients people to the same place. If Maria and Isaac can agree on the role and place of sex in their relationship, as part of a broad look at where they see themselves in a few months and what dimensions of their relationship they both want to work on and improve, they will be much closer to having a healthy relationship and a healthy sex life. They will have stopped their ways of using power against one another and will begin to use power for common ends, in their sex lives and at other places in their relationship.

In the end, no two people have the same kinds and amounts of power, and we are all more accustomed to using coercive power to get our way than we are to using power with one another for common ends. In our sexual lives, this may result in continual miscommunications and tensions. But that is not inevitable, and we can find ways to achieve greater mutuality and equality when it comes to our use of power. Indeed, we can move away from focusing on the power of the individual, which pits us against one another too often, and work on developing the power of the couple.

With this exploration of sexual power, we end our presentation of our ten puzzle pieces. In the next and final chapter of the book, we will list these ten, for ease of reference, and then begin to look at some of the ways we might assemble answers to them that answer your overall question: Should I have sex?

Questions for Reflection and Discussion

1. Where do you feel powerful, and where do you feel powerless? Given the various discussions in this chapter, where would you say your feelings are correct, and where are they probably incorrect?
2. Have you been a victim of coercive sexual power? What were the circumstances? How did it affect you? How and where have you sought healing?
3. Have you used sexual power coercively? What were the circumstances? How and where have you sought healing for doing that? Have you sought forgiveness?
4. Where have you seen sexual power used constructively and mutually? Has that shaped your own sexual life? Why or why not?
5. If sexual power used mutually succeeds by being directed toward common ends, building better relationships along the way, are there common sexual ends that we as a society could undertake that would benefit all of us?

PART 2 Solving the Puzzle

Chapter 11

Putting the Pieces Together
and Solving the Puzzle

I wish it were possible to sit down at this point with each reader individually to talk about his or her unique responses to the various questions asked here. After all, no two of you will assemble the puzzle pieces in the same way. Since individual conversations are impossible, I'm going to give you a look at four different solutions to the puzzle. Each of the scenarios in this chapter is about a twenty-something trying to decide whether to have sex. None of these composite portraits will look exactly like you, but it is very likely that one or more of them will overlap with you in significant ways.

I recommend that you read all four of these scenarios in order to continue to develop your perspective on the positive and negative dimensions of the choice before you. Each of the individuals depicted here makes a thoughtful, though obviously imperfect, case for a particular point of view. Your analysis of each scenario, which will be aided by the questions that follow it, should contribute meaningfully to your own decisions. In case you wish to read the scenarios out of order, here are the puzzle solutions at which the characters arrive:

- Debbie: "I don't believe in God, but there is something spiritually important about sex, and I'm not ready to have it again."
- Pat: "I'm Christian, and I'm waiting for marriage."
- Sarah: "I'm Christian, and I think sex with good friends is acceptable."
- Alex: "Sex should be reserved for times when we are in love."

Before examining these solutions, let's be sure we have the puzzle pieces on the table before us. Here they are in question form:

1. Informed consent: what do you need to know?
2. How will you treat other people?
3. In what kind of relationship do you want or need to be?

    4. If you do not wish to become pregnant, how will you prevent it?
    5. What if you become pregnant?
    6. Have you made any promises?
    7. What do God (or the idea of God) and the Bible have to offer?
    8. Why do you want to have sex?
    9. Would anyone be affected?
  10. What kind of power is involved?

Debbie

Debbie's view is, "I don't believe in God, but there is something spiritually important about sex, and I'm not ready to have it again." Let's see how she got there.

Debbie considers herself to be "spiritual but not religious." She enjoyed church when she was a child, but problems in her family church and the divorce of her parents drove her away from God and religious practices of all kinds. She called herself an atheist for a while, but in the last couple of years, she has started to have a sense that there is more to the world than we can see. She doesn't know what it is, but she thinks the many religions of the world are trying to find out. By calling herself "spiritual," she means that she thinks there might be layers of meaning in the world, meanings that are given to us, beyond us and not created by our choices and desires, meanings that people try to capture with their talk of God and gods. She is actively trying to discover whether any of the many faith traditions can help her to articulate what she senses.

Debbie was not sure where to begin constructing her puzzle. After reading the puzzle-piece chapters, though, the one idea she couldn't get out of her mind was chapter 7's suggestion that the idea of God functioned to orient believers to something permanent, good, and whole; she wondered if this could be said for her growing idea that the meaning of sex was somehow beyond us. She didn't think she could answer this fully without more time and study, but she thought what she was reaching for might be defined using the word "good." It was pretty clear, Debbie thought, that goodness isn't permanent in the sense of outweighing the bad in her life or in the world at any given moment, but she found herself hoping that what we see isn't the entire story and that good somehow wins out in the end. The idea that the world is pulling us toward good and fighting against bad felt right to her somehow, and she thought maybe we are supposed to do the same thing in our own lives, to work on being good in the face of the endless temptations to do otherwise. Maybe this struggle was our part in the world's drama.

Thinking about good and evil reminded Debbie of the notion of foster-ing good in chapter 2. More than just not harming people, Debbie wanted to help people, to make a positive difference in the world. She heard people talk about leaving the world better than we found it, and if anything defined her life right now, it was that sentiment. She hoped that people's days would be better because of their encounters with her: that's how she wanted to treat people. At the same time, she wasn't sure she could sacrifice much for any-one else at this point; after all, she was really just trying to get her own life in order. Maybe a little sacrifice, she thought, but certainly nothing like the Good Samaritan. Frankly, this bothered her, as she knew how much others had sacrificed for her, but maybe that was another aspect of the world's chal-lenge to her, she thought. Maybe being bothered that she couldn't give more was a sign that she was being invited not only to make the world a little better but also to give as much of herself as she could to the process. She could give something today, and maybe a little more tomorrow. Debbie couldn't find a way to resolve these questions of her role in the world, so she decided to move on to puzzle piece three.

Debbie had had sex with a boyfriend in high school and with five people in college, but her views were changing, and she wasn't sure what kind of relationship she thought she needed to be in now. She realized that she didn't have to keep having sex just because she had done it before, so she had recently been abstaining and trying to figure things out. Frankly, though, she really missed sex. The times she had sex in college were unfulfilling emo-tionally, but they were pretty "hot" otherwise. She loved to be caressed and kissed, and the orgasms she often had from oral sex were great. But she felt as though she was looking for something more lasting, more meaningful, and she was sure that some of her partners had been looking only for sex. On the other hand, Debbie knew being married wasn't the key for her; indeed, she really had never gotten close to marriage and didn't know whether she even wanted to marry. She felt herself being pushed toward the mutual love standard, but she knew that would be a very difficult commitment for her to make. She knew she could do other things besides have vaginal intercourse, if she was in a relationship that wasn't mutually loving yet, though she had to admit that even oral sex and mutual masturbation were starting to seem more meaningful to her than they once did. Was she going to have to abstain from those, too? Could she honestly say she needed to be in a mutually loving rela-tionship, or even a loving one, before she would do anything intensely sexual again? She didn't know, but she was beginning to sense that "I don't know" was getting to be one of her favorite responses to these puzzle questions, and that bothered her. It seemed as though the things she had been doing over the last few years didn't really fit with her current thoughts and feelings, especially since she couldn't even seem to identify her real thoughts and feelings. Maybe sex was just not for her anytime soon. Thinking that was at least a kind of conclusion, she moved to the pregnancy issues.

This one was easy. There was no way in hell she was ready to be pregnant now, thought Debbie. She didn't have a career, had no money to speak of, was living with a bunch of friends, and was working as a waitress to make ends meet. She enjoyed being a waitress; she enjoyed her friends. On the whole, she was pretty happy, but she certainly was not ready to devote her life to a child, especially when she had already realized she wasn't much into sacrificing right now. Debbie had also promised herself long ago that she would never be a single mom; her parents' divorce had created some very unstable times for her, and she vowed that her home would be a stable one before there were any kids in it. Since she knew abortion and adoption would be out for her, she either had to abstain from sex or be very sure about her birth control method. That didn't seem too difficult, since she had been on the pill before and had no trouble taking it regularly. She also typically required her partners to wear a condom, which lessened the possibility of STI transmission.

The real question for Debbie when it came to pregnancy and birth control was whether she wanted to go back on the pill. One thing she knew about herself for sure was that if she was on the pill and ended up in a position where she could have sex, she would probably do it. In her experience, once clothes started coming off, she didn't have a lot of will power. She knew she had to keep this one in mind as she thought about what she planned to do in the future.

Debbie thought the universe was a basically good place, and she knew she wanted to foster good for herself and others, and she knew she didn't want to be pregnant. She wondered why she was having such a hard time figuring out whether to have sex. What's the big deal about going back on the pill and having some fun, she wondered? The big deal, she realized, was that it just didn't quite feel right to her. There was something about sex that seemed to have more meaning to it than she could encounter in a quick hookup or even some steady sex with a good friend. In some way, she felt as though she was betraying herself by having emotionally disengaged sex with people.

The notion of betrayal reminded Debbie of the many promises that others had made to her in her life that had been broken. From around the time of her parents' divorce, she had become determined always to keep her promises. She hadn't really made any explicit promises to herself, but she wondered if her new awareness about the kind of meaning she sought out of life and sex was the beginning of a promise that was at least implicit. Sex was taking on an air of mystery to her that she couldn't quite explain, but it seemed to her as though that very air of mystery carried some kind of promise within it. If her intent was to cooperate with the good in the world, how could she not listen to her conscience?

Finally, although Debbie didn't think power issues had much to do with her, she decided she might as well take on that final question. She was aware of one situation in her past where she had been manipulated into having sex by someone who threatened to leave her, and this manipulation had lasted for a couple of months before she got up the courage to leave him. She also recognized one time where she had used someone just for sex and ended up really hurting him. The first person she didn't speak to anymore; in the second case, she had apologized a couple of years after the short fling, and she and her then-partner were now on pretty good terms. In reviewing the power chapter, Debbie noted that she had never thought much about ways coercive power might be built into us because of the society we live in. Frankly, this one scared her, because she started to wonder what sex was all about and whether she could ever have it again. Individual instances of the use of power, she thought, were pretty easy to discern, but coercive power that is socially embedded would be extremely difficult to see. Was all sex a power exchange of some sort? Was it an expression of abusive power? If so, she was pretty sure that she, as a woman, was on the losing end of it. Just one more thing she would have to think about, she told herself.

Debbie prided herself on her thinking abilities and on the "voice" of her heart to tell her what was right and what was wrong, but when she tried to put all of the puzzle pieces together, she realized how many of them she was not ready to take a stand on. She couldn't figure out what she thought or felt about the kind of relationships in which she wanted to be having sex, the meaning of sex, whether to go on the pill, whether she was making a promise to herself by way of her conscience; she wasn't sure of much of anything, she thought. She decided there were only two choices here: she could just forget all this stuff and enjoy having sex with people, or she could not have sex until she had sorted out more of the pieces and figured out what sex meant to her. The first option appealed to her in part because of the good times she had had with sex and the fact that she couldn't always bring herself to think that sex was such a big deal. On the other hand, if she was honest with herself, she wasn't always happy that she had made herself so vulnerable with some of her sexual partners, and she also felt as though if she actually wanted to foster good in the world she was going to have to start thinking about life and not just wandering through it blindly.

In the end, Debbie decided that she just wasn't ready to be having sex now. She knew her friends and roommates would keep doing what they were doing, and she didn't have any sense that she needed to try to convince them to live life her way, but she also knew that she was just way too confused about too many things to make a decision about sex that flowed from both her mind and her heart. "I don't believe in God," she concluded, "but there is something spiritually important about sex, and I'm not ready to have it again."

Questions for Reflection and Discussion

1. Does Debbie have to make not having sex a rule for her life? Couldn't having sex *sometimes* foster good (intimacy, orgasm, connection), so that she just looks at each opportunity as it presents itself?
2. It sounds as though Debbie is making her decision in isolation. Where might she look for help in trying to answer some of her questions?
3. Debbie argues that she wants her decision to have sex to be in accord with both her mind and her heart. Where do you see these two components at work in Debbie's process? Which one of them wins out in the end? Do you lean toward one or the other—head or heart? Why?
4. Why does uncertainty about what we want to do often mean not doing it? How does or should uncertainty shape our moral lives, if at all?

Pat

Pat's view is, "I'm Christian, and I'm waiting for marriage." Let's see how he got there.

Pat has not had sex and doesn't plan to until and unless he gets married, and his current girlfriend feels the same way. They don't know whether marriage is in their future, but they do love each other, and they continue to grow closer in many ways. They pray and sometimes attend church together. They have fun hiking in the summer and skiing in the winter. They share a love of music and photography. They are able to talk to each other about everything, almost as if they have known each other for decades. They enjoy sharing the ups and downs of their days with one another: Pat works in a bank, and his girlfriend is trying to make a living as a photographer, though neither of them plans on doing what they are doing now for a lifetime. They kiss, hold hands, and occasionally cuddle and nap together, but that is the extent of their sexual sharing. Pat sometimes reflects on how frustrating it can be not to do more, and he jokes with her that masturbation is his best friend; still, though, he believes God wants sex to be reserved for marriage.

Pat was very disappointed when he read chapter 7. It seemed to him that the two views there of God and of the Bible were both extreme, one in the direction of what he calls fundamentalism, the other in the direction of what he calls secular humanism. One turned the Bible into the direct words of God while the other seemed to contribute nothing but a few broad principles that could be generated by any number of religious or secular traditions. Pat considers both of these rather narrow and misguided, even if widespread, forms of real Christian faith. He considers God to be less of a lawgiver telling us how to live our lives (either generally or specifically), and more of our creator and guide, who has envisioned for us a quality of life that fulfills us. God invites us to participate in this fulfilling life, calling us to be faithful to God and to one another as we are transformed by our encounters with God in Christ, both through the Bible and elsewhere.

What does this mean for his thinking about sex? For Pat, the meaning of sex is not to be found in some particular set of rules, although maybe some rules can capture bits and pieces of how we ought to live. The problem, in Pat's eyes, is this very notion of "bits and pieces." Christian moral life, Pat thinks, is a matter of asking ourselves whether we are, in every way and place, being faithful to the leading of God and the vision of abundant life to which God is leading us; it isn't about dividing life up into little bits and pieces and trying to find or create rules, general or specific, that apply to them.

Pat is the first to admit that applying this view to an issue such as whether to have sex is no easy task. There is no straightforward answer to it, and neither the simple "don't" approach of biblical fundamentalists nor the permissiveness of the love principle quite encapsulates a strong sexual ethic. Instead, we have to be living in continual relationship with God, Christ, and the church, allowing ourselves to be pushed, prodded, and called toward a richer and more faithful life. What this means cannot be known outside of the living of it.

There was a time when this would have seemed like gibberish to Pat, but these days it seems like a new and refreshing truth. The necessity of acting and making decisions helps us to keep the theory in mind. We still have to have sex or not have sex, for example. We have to live in economically simple or economically possessive ways. We have to pray daily or not. We have to support gay marriage or not. We have to shape a married life like that outlined in Ephesians or not. For all of these, we have to decide which way to go; life doesn't just happen.

Nor is it a matter of agreement, at least among Christians Pat knows, about which of the choices in any of these cases is the most life-fulfilling and faithful one. In the case of sex, though, he has decided, and his girlfriend has agreed, that marriage is the place where sex can be most free, where long-term exploration of what fidelity really means is possible, and where, at least ideally, the greatest transformation of one's sexual life can occur.

Without the insecurities and impermanence of unmarried sex, people are free to explore what sex is all about in conversation with God, the Bible, and the church. That, Pat thinks, is about the best job of understanding the Christian life that he can do at this point.

Although Pat considers his views on God and the Bible to be enough to tell him what to do about having sex, these aren't the only puzzle pieces that shape his view. There are at least three others (besides the obvious one that he wants to be in a married relationship when he has sex). First, Pat thinks it is wrong to treat people the way he often sees people treated when they have sex. The vast majority of the time, it seems to him, they are simply used for sex: so few are willing to wait until they make the final commitment of marriage, which means that people are having sex in situations of impermanence, leaving behind huge emotional wreckage.

Second, the reason Pat wants to have sex is to become one with someone, to "become one flesh," as the Bible puts it in its metaphorical way. The risks of becoming one and then ending up separating in divorce are high enough these days, Pat thinks, without adding other conditions under which similar separation can occur. If one of the purposes of sex, other than procreation, is the unity of one flesh, then sex is far more special than we usually give it credit for. Unity of two people is not, in Pat's view, a casual matter. If he is going to become one with someone, it is going to be with one person and one person only, not one person now and another person tomorrow or next year.

The third additional reason Pat wants to wait until he is married to have sex is that he has expressed to many friends his belief that this is the way he believes we should live. While he knows they will love him the same whether he holds to what he considers to be a promise or not, he also knows they will be disappointed because of the importance of his model for him. He tries to be a model of faithfulness and finds that this has actually kept him from giving into temptation on a number of occasions. Although he doubts that this sense of responsibility would actually keep him from having sex were it not for the Christian foundation on which his views rest, he still considers his promises to others to be important.

Questions for Reflection and Discussion

1. Pat thinks his view of the Bible and God is better than the two views (ends of the continuum) presented in chapter 7. Which of the three views do you think is the best, and why?

2. Is there any good reason for Pat to be thinking about his friends when he ponders whether or not to have sex? Do you look to any of your friends as "models of faithfulness"? Are there friends whose actions or choices can really disappoint you?
3. Pat believes that sex in marriage is somehow freer and safer than sex outside of marriage. How can he make that argument? Do you believe his argument works? Why or why not?
4. Take Pat's way of thinking about the Christian moral life, and try to apply it to other sexual behaviors. Consider oral sex, perhaps. Would Pat think this should wait for marriage, too? Do you agree? Why or why not?

Sarah

Sarah's view is, "I'm Christian, and I think sex with good friends is acceptable." Let's see how she got there.

"Yes," Sarah says when asked, "I am a Christian, though there are probably a lot of people who don't think so. But I believe in God, and I do my best to live a good life. I think Jesus is a model for all of us. I don't go to church much, but that's mostly a matter of habit. And I don't suppose I get all that much out of it. God and I have a good relationship without Sunday morning church."

Sarah grew up in the church. She went with her parents most weeks, was active in the youth group for years, preached on Youth Sunday, and even thought for a while about being a pastor. She didn't go as much once she got to college, except when she was home, but she occasionally went to a Christian fellowship group, read her Bible pretty regularly with her roommate, and prayed every night. Now, in her senior year, she is preparing to take a year off before going to some graduate school; she hasn't yet decided whether to study for the ministry.

Sarah began getting sexual in high school when she first started going to parties and dating. It was a gradual thing, and by the time she arrived at college, she was thinking about having sex with her boyfriend from back home. They didn't and broke up after she had been at school for a couple of months. Sarah partied a bit, messed around here and there, and then met Josh. They became good friends, spent a lot of time together, started spending nights together, and ended up having sex about three months later. This went on for most of the next year. There was some initial interest on both of their parts in a steady, long-term relationship, but that didn't last long. They had been "friends with benefits," she supposed, if someone wanted to label it. Neither of them was ready to make a long-term commitment.

Josh transferred after their sophomore year, and Sarah didn't see him again for a long time. By the time she did, he had a girlfriend, so sex with Sarah was out. She had brief sexual relationships with three people after that, two of them overlapping by a couple of months; any of these folks might have become real relationships for her, but they just didn't. She felt good, though, about both the sex and the quality of the friendships. Both were terrific, and the friendships were lasting, even though the sexual aspects faded in time as the parties figured out they were really in the "just friends" category.

Sarah considers her mom her best friend, someone to whom she can tell anything and still be loved. Her mom doesn't like the fact that Sarah has sex outside of a long-term and committed relationship, though she accepts that it's Sarah's life to live. One night when Sarah was home on break, her mom asked her how she thought about sex and with whom she had sex. Sarah gave a quick answer, but then pondered the puzzle pieces over the next few weeks. The next time she was home, Sarah gave her mom a more complete answer.

She started with one of her mom's big concerns—pregnancy and STIs. "First of all, I get Depo-Provera shots, mom, so I'm not going to become pregnant," she said. "If I did, I would probably have an abortion." In her view, an early abortion can be justified by the freedom God gave us to direct our own lives when pregnancy is unwanted. Also, she told her mom, she always demands that her partners wear condoms, so she's not really worried about either pregnancy or STI's. And since her mother took her to get the Gardasil vaccination years ago, she feels she is pretty well protected.

Sarah finds it a little harder to explain why she feels that friendship is a fine place for sex. In the end, she decides that she just doesn't see any big mysteries involved when it comes to sex. It's a natural, healthy way for two people to express their caring for one another and have fun together. She wouldn't have sex with someone she didn't trust, of course, partly because sex does make her vulnerable and partly because she also wants some emotional intimacy from people, but she thinks it is just irrational to act in any other way. She can't figure out why, other than impaired or uninformed consent, anyone would have sex with someone they don't know well enough to trust. Who wants to be lying naked and vulnerable with someone who doesn't care?

Sarah supposes her general understanding of sex is shaped by her views on God and the Bible. Sarah values the Bible and thinks every Christian should take it seriously. She thinks the Bible was written by people describing what they took to be their experiences of God, which often meant blessing their own views and actions with the language of divine authority. If a society doesn't want people to "fornicate" and wants to keep its current social structure, those things will appear in its sacred text, not with any intention to deceive or control but simply because that's the way the writers understand their own ways: as ordained and blessed by God. The stories in the Bible, Sarah thinks, are the ones that continue to help Christians make sense of who they are and how they think they should live, but those stories are not to be valued above the current experiences of faithful people. To put this another way, when the Bible reaches high moral standards of love and justice, that's great, and she thinks that's what Jesus represents; when it doesn't fit with our best contemporary models and other important religious ones, Sarah thinks these ideas can be tossed. When it comes to sex, Sarah knows what the Bible says, and she thinks there are good reasons to suppose that some of the authors were opposed to sex outside of marriage, but that doesn't carry much weight with Sarah. Sex is, as far as she can tell, biologically for procreation, but we have helped to make it for recreation, too, by inventing reliable birth control methods and redesigning the whole idea of families. God gave us the power to re-create ourselves to some extent, and we have: sex can now be for fun. In her experience, sex can be rich and joyful. It has given her encounters with reality and other people that she thinks might even be hints of the divine.

But even fun sex still can't be had with just anyone, thinks Sarah. Because of the vulnerability that's attached to it, there has to be some trust involved. By trust, she means that she can rely on the person not to talk about their time together, not to hurt her, not to run away if something happens, to spend time with her and not just screw her, things like that. Her reasons for having sex are to be open and really encounter one of her friends in a special way.

And, as Sarah tries to assure her mom, she doesn't rush into sexual involvement. She takes seriously the issue of real, true informed consent. She wants to be sure her partner understands that they are committed friends but not committed lovers. If they fall in love, that's fine, but if they meet other people with whom they want a different kind of relationship, being honest about it is the key to the friendship continuing. Does it hurt when that happens? Sure it does, for a while. But that's a natural part of caring about someone and part of the intimacy of sex. Thinking about what she wants to know to fully consent, trust is primary. This includes knowing where the person stands about sex, but she also wants to know that she has some real connection with the person. Mutual understanding of the meaning of sex is part of the right kind of connection.

As long as everyone is honest, Sarah doesn't mind it if the people she sees and sleeps with are also sleeping with other people, and she has occasionally been seeing and sleeping with more than one person at a time. She knows that not everyone can handle these kinds of relationships; they get too possessive and emotionally attached, and for her to allow that would not be loving. She insists on not hurting anyone; if she has any inkling that her partners cannot handle a fun, mature, caring, trusting sexual relationship, she won't have sex with them. That seems to her to be an appropriate reflection of God's love for all of us.

Questions for Reflection and Discussion

1. What would you expect to be the major places of disagreement between Sarah and Pat, the two Christians in our scenarios? What is it about Sarah's worldview, in your eyes, that enables her to call herself a Christian? Are there places she seems to you not to have understood her own faith?
2. Sarah relies a lot on trust and friendship in choosing her sexual partners. What are trust and friendship, and how would you evaluate them as appropriate standards for making sexual decisions? How long does it take to establish sufficient trust to have sex with someone?
3. Have you ever had a "friend with benefits"? Did the benefits change the friendship in any ways? When the benefits ended, did the friendship end? Why or why not?
4. Many would argue that Sarah's view of abortion, which appears to be grounded in our God-given freedom to control our lives, ignores some very important moral questions. What do you think?
5. Why is Sarah the first of our scenarios to pay attention to the informed consent issue? How does she understand it?

Alex

Alex's view is, "Sex should be reserved for times when you are in love." Let's see how he got there.

Alex doesn't consider himself to have any religious or spiritual convictions whatsoever, though some of his friends would disagree, as he is one of the most honest and upright people they know. He doesn't believe in God, but if spirituality has to do with one's ethics, they say, he's definitely spiritual. Alex mostly thinks his friends have some need to fit him into the categories with which they are comfortable.

From Alex's point of view, life is about love. That's what his father has always said, and everyone respects his father. In talking with his dad about it over the years, Alex learned that his dad got this view from *his* dad, Alex's grandfather. Alex thought the idea meant something a little different to his grandfather, perhaps something like "Be a good neighbor to the whole community, and treat everyone with equal respect." To his father, though, "Life is about love" seemed to mean something like "Treat others the way you want to be treated." That's how Alex saw his dad act with colleagues and family, including Alex and Alex's mother. Alex tried to put these things together in developing the meaning of his own life, and he had decided that acting lovingly meant something like always treating people with respect and with their best interests in mind.

Of course, Alex loved the people he had sex with in a very different way than he might love his colleagues or other members of his community, but the overall meaning was still there. He has only had sex with two people, one in college and one a couple of years later. The last of these relationships ended about four months ago now, and Alex has started to hang out with his friends more again, including a couple of women he finds interesting. Sex, for him, could legitimately become more intimate the deeper one's friendship or relationship grows, but truly active concern for the well-being of the woman has to be present before Alex will have intercourse. There is no real mystery to this, as far as Alex is concerned. Women sometimes tell him that having vaginal intercourse is in some sense giving all of themselves, and he feels the same. Such complete giving really has to wait for its right time, and that time is when love is present.

One friend is pushing Alex on the question of why sex doesn't have to wait for marriage. If it really means giving all, his friend challenges, then isn't marriage the appropriate relationship for it? Alex doesn't think so. Certainly marriage is a different kind of commitment, maybe even a different level of commitment, but it isn't necessarily more intense; it doesn't necessarily mean one is more committed to the other person's well-being. He can't imagine actually feeling more intensely for any woman than he had for his former girlfriends. Yes, those relationships ended, and he wasn't even friends with them any longer. He still feels that sex with them was appropriate, however, because love was present at the time.

Does the love have to be mutual? Yes. That's what makes the relationship so deep. It doesn't make sense to have sex with someone you love who feels something less for you; that is just setting yourself up to be hurt. And it is even worse to have sex with someone you don't love but who loves you. That is just abusive, as far as Alex is concerned. It is using the other person for your own sexual ends. When a woman once said she didn't care how he felt about her, that she just wanted to know what it was like to have sex with him, Alex didn't believe she was aware of what she was saying, and he refused. One couldn't volunteer to be used, thought Alex, though he hadn't said it. She was not thoughtfully consenting, in his view.

Alex thinks he can move through the puzzle pieces fairly quickly, with love as his guide. It isn't loving to have sex with someone when you aren't

both fully informed about your motivations and other influential life circumstances; informed consent is a necessity. One has to be completely faithful
to one's promises, certainly, and one's motivation to have sex should be the
desire to share love with another human being who loves you. Obviously, it's
loving to protect oneself and the other person from STIs, and absolute pregnancy prevention is a necessity. Alex had always used a condom, and all of
his girlfriends had used something that was at least 99 percent effective. Alex
would have considered it his responsibility, of course, to care for any child
that resulted from his having sex; nothing else would be loving.

The puzzle piece that stymies Alex a bit is the whole discussion of power.
His problem here is that, while it is pretty clear to him what love means when
it is a matter of one individual loving another, or even one individual loving
a group, how love can work in a social climate of coercive power took him a
while to sort out. This is what he came up with, though he feels pretty tentative about it.

If coercive power is acting in a way that overrides the free choice of
another person, then Alex considers love to be the opposite. Love completely
respects, even tries to enhance, the free choice of the other person. But suppose coercion is so embedded that there are deep power distinctions between
members of society, distinctions that call into question whether the choices
people believe are free are truly free. If, for instance, men have power that
women do not have simply because they are men in a patriarchal society, can
sex ever be freely chosen by women, or is it always in some way coerced?
Alex truly has no idea, but he thinks if anything can make a difference, it is a
love that respects the woman enough to give her the time and space to make
her own choices and to respect whatever choice she makes. Other than that
and doing everything he can do not to manipulate or try to in any way coerce
the woman he loves, Alex doesn't know what else to do. But he does consider the problem to be serious enough to commit himself to thinking about
it in the near future and acting on what he discovers. Is love the antidote to a
coercive society, or is love itself corrupted by that society? And what are the
implications for sexual behavior of answering this question?

Questions for Reflection and Discussion

1. Does spirituality or being spiritual have to do primarily with our ethics?
2. Is Alex talking about love or being in love? Is there a difference, in your
   view? If there is, how would you express it, and how does it relate to

having sex? How do you see the roles of reason and of feeling in loving someone?

3. Alex clearly thinks his notion of love helps him to weave his way through the questions very quickly. Are you as confident as he is about that? Why or why not? Are there particular questions, other than puzzle piece six, where you think Alex would get hung up?

4. Alex's view that other people are to be treated in a particular way comes from his family. When you think about your basic view of how people should be treated, where does it come from? What ways of living have you adopted from your upbringing and what ways have you rejected? Why?

5. Is it really wrong to have sex with someone who feels differently about you than you feel about him or her? Why or why not?

Conclusion

These four scenarios are intended to inspire you to think more deeply and more fully about what it means to combine the puzzle pieces we have explored into your solution to the question of whether you should have sex. They are sketches only, but they are sufficient to give you some understanding of both the complexity of the issues raised in this book as well as a few of the many shapes a coherent answer might take. Each one of the composite characters with a starring role in one of the scenarios brings a different background, set of biases, and sexual history to the table. They begin their reflective process in different places and vary in the questions they choose to address in great detail and the ones they believe they need to address only briefly. Each person believes she or he has good reasons to act in the ways described, and our position in this book is that there are things to recommend each view. The question we always face is whether we can give good reasons to support our chosen way of life and whether this way is as true and as faithful to us and to the needs of our world as possible. With respect to the question it asks—Should I have sex?—I think and hope that the approach offered here can guide you to your own truest and most faithful answer.

Appendix

Questions and Responses

*I*n various conversations with students and friends before and during the writing of this book, many questions came up over and over again. I was able to work responses to many of them into the main chapters of the book; others I decided to address briefly in this separate section. I have called what I say here "responses" instead of "answers" because I am not trying to give a once-for-all definitive solution to any question. Mostly, these are simply some ideas with which to start as you search for your own answers. Here are the top fifteen questions I have received and my responses in one paragraph each.

1. How important is sex?
That's an excellent question. Sex has been important in my life, though not as important as love and companionship. It is probably not as important as our hormones and culture try to convince us when we are young, but it ties in to enough other things—self-worth, vulnerability, body image, need for love and touch—that it is an aspect of life well worth spending time thinking about and working on. In the end, the most important thing is to be sure you find healthy outlets for your sexual energy; when you are coupled, the most important thing is that you and your partner come to an understanding of its role in your life together. Agreement on that is more important than any external evaluation of its role in life, and honest and accepting communication with each other about your sex life will save you countless hours of mostly ridiculous but sometimes very painful argument.

2. If I have had sex once, does it matter whether I keep doing it?
This is *the* most asked question by the students with whom I study and work, and the answer is, Yes, it matters. It is your choice whether or not you have sex; this is true the first time and the thousandth. (If you were forced to have sex on some occasion, it is maybe even more important that you recognize

subsequent sexual activity as being your choice.) There is nothing about having sex once that obligates you or fates you to having it another time. What matters about having sex is not whether you have had it before but whether the next time is the result of your informed, healthy, and wise choice.

3. Does God trust me enough to make my own decisions?

Speaking for God is always risky. I hope the previous chapters have suggested to you that there are many ways to think of God, even within Christianity. If we were having a real conversation, I would respond to this question by asking you who God is for you, and we would develop our answer from there. In my view, our apparent freedom *requires* us to make our own decisions. At the same time, God's gift of freedom comes with God's invitation to us to act in some ways rather than others. The "right" ways are those that express and enable the love of God, love of neighbor, and the well-being of all. We cannot do better than to attempt this in all we do, sexual and otherwise.

4. Can Christian decision making be individual, or do we all have to act the same?

Christians stand before God both alone and together, both individually and in community with one another. In some sense, then, Christian decision making must be individual (*you* have to choose), but in order to be Christian (as opposed to humanist, Taoist, or something else), it will also have some features in common with other Christian choices. To go to what I take to be the heart of the question, people who wish to identify themselves as Christians will differ in their moral decisions and actions, but they will make their decisions out of their engagement with the kinds of sources discussed in chapter 7. Some Christians will stand before God and in their communities having made the reasonable and faithful choice to wait until they are married to have sex, and other Christians will stand before God and in their communities having made the reasonable and faithful choice to have sex while being unmarried. To my mind, both decisions can reflect and aim at the wholeness and well-being of creation. We do not all have to act the same when we act in love and faithfulness.

5. Is there only one person for me?

This is usually a theological question, asking whether God has a partner in store for us, someone who, in God's master plan, is our soul mate. A complete response would, again, require us to examine our assumptions. Among other things, we would need to ponder how many events and people God would have to shape in order to get every person to the right place where he or she could meet and fall in love with his or her intended mate. It seems to me, however, that experience suggests the answer to the question is no. I have heard many people claim to have met "the one," only to split up a month or a decade later. What should we make of that? Were they wrong when the relationship began, or when it ended? Were they so confident that this was the right person that they didn't work at the relationship? Personally, I find it freeing to suppose that there are many people with whom we might build good and fulfilling lives, but I know not everyone will agree.

6. What about vibrators, lotions, and other sex aids?

The question sometimes conveys a worry that such aids might corrupt the sanctity of sex, and such questions are always worth taking seriously. How we respond to such a worry will depend on our view of the meaning of sex. In the end, aids that enhance sexual experience and don't cause harm of any kind seem innocent enough, unless they violate what you take sex to be about. There's nothing wrong with experimenting or even pushing your comfort level a bit if you feel completely safe with your partner, but don't be pushed into trying something with which you are seriously uncomfortable, and never let yourself be harmed, emotionally or physically.

7. Where can I find help if I need it?

First, please do not hesitate to reach out for whatever kind of help you need. Being hurt, ashamed, embarrassed, or worried can stop us from reaching out, and that frequently just makes things worse. Once you are determined to get help, where you turn will depend a lot on what kind of help you need. You might talk with a counselor in your area or on your campus. If you are part of a church, you might call your pastor. Parents and trusted friends can be good resources, depending on the issues involved. Your local pharmacy has over-the-counter morning-after pills, which act a lot like birth control pills, but are intended for use within a short time following unprotected sex. (You might visit a site such as www.mayoclinic.com/health/morning-after-pill/AN00592 for more information.) Planned Parenthood generally does pregnancy counseling and testing, and www.plannedparenthood.org offers a wealth of information. If you think you have an STI, call your doctor for an appointment; if you don't have a doctor, ask someone you trust to recommend a good one, and call to make an appointment soon. Most of the people I have mentioned will keep your questions and information confidential, but don't be afraid to talk with them about this if it is of concern to you.

8. How do I get over the pain of a random hookup?

The first issue here is to identify what is causing the pain. Are you hurting because you had a random hookup after you promised yourself that you wouldn't? Because sexual intimacy means more to you than your actions show? Because of the person you hooked up with, or because the sex was unprotected? Because it was the first time you had sex, and you didn't want your first time to look like this? Because you found out that the sex didn't mean the same thing to you and the person you had sex with? There is no way to prescribe briefly how to get over any of these things, but in general, you will want to understand why you did what you did so that you can figure out how not to put yourself in the same position again, and you will want to work on forgiving yourself. If your random hookup was wrong for you to do, then learning more about why you did it should help you accept your fallibility (as a human being) and begin to move on. The previous question suggests some helpful resources in case you want to explore them.

9. How do I *not* have sex when everyone around me seems to be?

When everyone around us appears to be doing any given thing and we have decided not to participate, it can be very difficult. Feeling left out, excluded, and alone can be hard, even if it is by our own choosing. The two major things I can think of to say are, first, that the situation is not a permanent one and might best be considered a kind of test of our character, and, second, that even though making new friends can be difficult, there are certainly people who have chosen the path you have chosen. Is there a way you can spend sufficient time with them to at least help you feel less lonely? Again, don't hide; reach out to talk with someone so you can get some needed companionship.

10. Is masturbation okay?

Sure. Having said that, though, it is important to add that many Christians disagree, in part on the grounds that God's intentions for sex are procreation and union, neither of which is possible with masturbation. If you apply the relevant questions in this book to the question, however, you might come out in a different place, Christian or not. Are you harming someone else? If, for example, you are having a sexual relationship but masturbate so much that the relationship is harmed, that is obviously a problem. If you find yourself virtually addicted to the pleasure of masturbation, that is obviously a problem. If you engage in it as a healthy sexual practice that doesn't reach the level of harm or obsession, then it seems easily justifiable, morally speaking.

11. How should I think about pornography?

I like the way this question is phrased, because we need to be thinking about pornography. The first thing I would say about porn is that if you look at it, try looking at it with the eyes of a critical thinker and see what you learn. Also, listen to the experiences of your friends, especially female ones. I have now heard so many troubling stories from so many people that it is not possible for me to buy into the notion that viewing porn is basically innocent adult fun. I've watched relationships end because the woman was disturbed by the amount of porn her partner watched; his promises to stop were never followed by the promised action. I've watched other relationships end because of the man's predilection for imitating the detached sex of pornographic movies or for making comments about his girlfriend's body relative to the last porn actress he saw. I've seen men realize that their difficulties in the bedroom were the result of a preoccupation with porn. These, of course, are occasional anecdotes and are concerned with the use of porn as opposed to the making of it, funding of it, and so forth, but they are common enough for us to be sure we don't take pornography lightly. It is important for each one of us to take seriously its impact on us if we view it, and its impact on our partners. Listening to one's partner talk about that impact may be the key to understanding. These days, pornography use among women is also rapidly increasing, which adds additional reflections on social power to our considerations.

12. What about group sex?

This question can provoke such outcry that it's worth asking where one is standing when asking it. Obviously, if you are asking from the point of view of someone who believes that all sex should be reserved for marriage, then, unless you are in favor of plural marriages, you have your answer. Suppose though you are asking from the point of view of someone who thinks sex can be appropriate with trusted friends or that all that is needed to justify sex is mutual consent. In that case, you could *logically* find group sex morally permissible. The key is to apply the other questions—about how to treat people, about promises, and about power, for instance. Again, the answer to the question will depend on your assessment of the meaning of sex and the rest of the issues discussed.

13. Is there such a thing as secondary virginity?

First, defining primary virginity is not an easy task. Is it a purely biological matter, or is it an emotional or spiritual state of innocence? The key to the question about secondary virginity, however, seems to be the worry about whether we can "take back" the sex we have had. If we have sex once or for a few years, can we stop and talk about ourselves as virgins again? Certainly we can change our behavior, and if it is helpful to talk about this change as secondary virginity, that seems reasonable. There is, however, another aspect of this question on which I want to take a more firm stand. To my mind, one cannot have one's virginity taken by assault or rape. Of course, if your personal experience is otherwise, I have no stake in arguing with you, but rape and sexual abuse are not about having sex, so if you were a virgin and were raped, I think you can take some of your power back by continuing to think of yourself as a virgin. Virginity ought to be considered something that can only be given, not taken by force. As a moral issue, I would consider someone a virgin until they choose to change that carefully defined state.

14. Why am I not comfortable with physical/emotional intimacy?

We all vary in our comfort with intimacy of various kinds. Much of the time, this stems from the ways in which intimacy was expressed to us in our childhood and the kinds of intimacy we saw our parents express then. Discomfort with touch or intimacy often means our childhood (which may well have been loving) was not very physically or emotionally connected or demonstrative. Another possibility is that we were abused in some way that makes such intimacy difficult for us, though that is not a conclusion we should jump to quickly. Sometimes, recognizing that our parents, for instance, never hugged in our presence lets us know why we have a difficult time with hugs, and that realization is all we need to move on. Sometimes, the issues are more serious, in which case we should find a good counselor. Sexual intimacy also requires a good bit of trust and vulnerability, and those are sometimes difficult to develop and easy to injure.

15. What about oral sex?

The development of sexual intimacy may be, and often is, thought of as a series of steps, behaviors that range from the less intimate to the more intimate. Putting your head on someone's shoulder or kissing him or her lightly might be seen as an early or less intimate step, and oral sex and sexual intercourse have typically been thought of as the most intimate steps. These days, we frequently hear reports about the trivialization of oral sex, which in effect means that it has become, for some, a much earlier step on the road of intimacy. Morally speaking, is this a good thing or a bad thing? More particularly, under what circumstances is oral sex right for you?

Many of the issues that we have explored in this book relate as much to oral sex as they do to intercourse, and pondering oral sex within the puzzle framework already provided should be helpful. How do you want to treat other people? In what kind of relationship do you want to be when you have oral sex? You cannot become pregnant through oral sex, of course, but you can contract or spread STIs; how does that factor into your decision? Many current reports of adolescent oral sex appear to be misuses of male power; is that relevant to your situation? Are you being coerced or coercing someone else? Perhaps the best short answer I can give to the question of "What about oral sex?" is to encourage you to use the framework you have already explored in this book to see whether oral sex is right or wrong for you.

Helpful Readings

*T*his is by no means a comprehensive list of important books related to sexual ethics. Instead, these are some of the books that I have found to be most helpful in thinking about some of the issues I have discussed in this book.

If you compare what I have written in these chapters with what is contained in the books on this list, you will find places of both agreement and disagreement. In thinking about significant issues, I try to read a broad range of material, including things with which I know I will disagree strongly.

Abramson, Paul R. *Sex Appeal: Six Ethical Principles for the 21st Century*. New York: Oxford University Press, 2010. This small and accessible book can be read on at least two levels. First and foremost, it presents six guiding principles for a safe, enjoyable, and kind sexual life. Second, embedded within each of the chapters are enough pointers to personal reflection and societal analysis to keep the reader engaged for a long time.

Ariely, Dan. *Predictably Irrational: The Hidden Forces That Shape Our Decisions*. Revised and expanded edition. New York: HarperCollins, 2008. Chapter 5, "The Influence of Arousal," recounts a small study in which college males predicted their sexual behavior very differently when they were aroused than they did when they were not aroused. When aroused, for instance, a much higher percentage said they would "tell a woman that you loved her to increase the chance that she would have sex with you" (107).

Barnes, William H. "Inspiration and Inerrancy," In *The Oxford Companion to the Bible*, edited by Bruce M. Metzger and Michael D. Coogan, 302–4. New York: Oxford University Press, 1993. The *Oxford Companion* is an excellent one-volume resource on things biblical. This brief article will inspire your thinking about biblical interpretation.

Beauchamp, Tom L., and James F. Childress. *Principles of Biomedical Ethics*. 5th ed. New York: Oxford University Press, Inc., 2001. Chapters 1, 8, and 9 are particularly helpful in thinking about morality itself; chapter 4 is a valuable discussion of the principle of not harming others.

Blank. Hanne. *Virgin: The Untouched History*. New York: Bloomsbury, 2007. This is a fascinating study of the invention of concepts of virginity.

Borowitz, Eugene B. *Choosing a Sex Ethic: A Jewish Inquiry*. New York: Schocken Books, 1969. This book has long been out of print, but it is one of the best on this list. Borowitz argues that there are several acceptable sex ethics: mutual consent, love, and marriage. He judges the marriage ethic to be the "most right" of these, as it most fully expresses who we are in relationship with one another and with God. You can see this book's influence on my own categories and way of thinking in chapter 3.

Cahill, Lisa Sowle. *Between the Sexes: Foundations for a Christian Ethics of Sexuality*. Philadelphia: Fortress Press, 1985. Cahill has done more recent work in the area, but this early work is the one I read. It is a careful and thoughtful reflection on doing Christian ethics and on centrally important biblical and historical arguments.

Carpenter, Laura M. *Virginity Lost: An Intimate Portrait of First Sexual Experiences*. New York: New York University Press, 2005. This engaging sociological study explores the different meanings attached to one's "first time."

Coelho, Paulo. *Eleven Minutes*. New York: Perennial, 2005. This is not always an emotionally easy novel to read, but it has consistently been a favorite of students as we explore good sex and bad sex.

Ellison, Marvin M. *Same-Sex Marriage? A Christian Ethical Analysis*. Cleveland: Pilgrim Press, 2004. This book does just what the title suggests: it argues within a Christian moral framework in favor of same-sex marriage.

Ellison, Marvin M., and Kelly Brown Douglas, eds. *Sexuality and the Sacred: Sources for Theological Reflection,* 2nd ed. Louisville, KY: Westminster John Knox Press, 2010. This updated and expanded edition of a popular anthology of essays about sexuality includes essays on abortion, homosexuality, eroticism, racism, and gender.

Farley, Margaret A. *Just Love: A Framework for Christian Sexual Ethics*. New York: Continuum, 2006. This is the newest "must read" in Christian sexual ethics. It includes historical and cross-cultural investigation and concludes with Farley's "just love" framework. It's not always an easy read but it is always a worthwhile one.

Feinberg, Joel. *The Moral Limits of the Criminal Law*. Vol. 1, *Harm to Others*. New York: Oxford University Press, 1984. If you are seeking a complex analysis of harm, this is a place to find it.

Freitas, Donna. *Sex & the Soul: Juggling Sexuality, Spirituality, Romance, and Religion on America's College Campuses*. New York: Oxford University Press, 2008. This book chronicles the results of a broad study in which students talk about their spiritual and sexual lives and the connections (or lack thereof) between them. Helpful both in the data it supplies and the wide range of issues discussed, it should be valuable for parents of college-bound young people.

Gilligan, Carol. *In a Different Voice: Psychological Theory and Women's Development*. Cambridge, MA: Harvard University Press, 1982. I was at Harvard Divinity School when this book came out, and it seemed to me everyone was walking around reading it. It's a classic in several fields and another "must-read." Gilligan reveals two different "voices" for ethical reflection and kicks off decades of widespread conversation about the "ethic of care." This ethical voice is most often, though not exclusively, associated with women.

González, Justo L. "How the Bible Has Been Interpreted in Christian Tradition." In *The New Interpreter's Bible: A Commentary in Twelve Volumes*. Edited by Leander Keck et al. Vol. 1, 83–106. Nashville: Abingdon Press, 1994. If you are interested in verse-by-verse commentary on the Bible, this is a good place to go. There are several articles in the first volume on interpretation, including this one.

Grenz, Stanley J. *Sexual Ethics: An Evangelical Perspective*. Louisville, KY: Westminster John Knox Press, 1990. This is a biblically based look at a wide range of sexual ethical issues. It's pretty dense in places, but it's worth taking slowly in order to understand what Grenz is saying.

Grossman, Maria, M.D. *Unprotected: A Campus Psychiatrist Reveals How Political Correctness in Her Profession Endangers Every Student*. New York: Sentinel, 2007. Perhaps the title speaks for itself. The author argues that students are not getting the information they need to stay safe and healthy.

Hollinger, Dennis P. *The Meaning of Sex: Christian Ethics and the Moral Life*. Grand Rapids: Baker Academic, 2009. Based in the Bible and various fundamental claims of the Christian faith, Hollinger argues that sex has a meaning and that its meaning is God given. He includes a discussion of a wide range of issues based on his Christian framework.

Jones, Abigail, and Marissa Miley. *Restless Virgins: Love, Sex, and Survival at a New England Prep School*. New York: William Morrow, 2007. Based on interviews, this is a look at some of the members of the high school class of 2005 at Milton Academy. The kinds of struggles and issues they face are worth reflection.

Lawler, Rev. Ronald, OFM Cap., Joseph Boyle Jr., and William E. May. *Catholic Sexual Ethics: A Summary, Explanation, & Defense*. 2nd ed. Huntington, IN: Our Sunday Visitor, 1998. Lawler et al. offer an excellent look at Catholic moral thinking on issues in sexual ethics.

Paul, Pamela. *Pornified: How Pornography Is Transforming Our Lives, Our Relationships, and Our Families*. New York: Henry Holt & Co., 2005. Porn is pervasive. This is a readable book for beginning to think about some of the troubling issues related to it.

Stepp, Laura Sessions. *Unhooked: How Young Women Pursue Sex, Delay Love and Lose at Both*. New York: Riverhead Books, 2007. The title explains the book. It's a helpful look at contemporary hookup culture.

Winner, Lauren F. *Real Sex: The Naked Truth about Chastity*. Grand Rapids: Brazos Press, 2005. Clear and easy to read, this is a popular and personal introduction to the conservative side of Christian thinking about sex.

Notes

Chapter 3—In What Kind of Relationship Do You Want or Need to Be?

1. I have been deeply influenced in this chapter and in my overall thinking on these matters by Rabbi Eugene B. Borowitz, *Choosing a Sex Ethic: A Jewish Inquiry* (New York: Schocken Books, 1969).

2. Barry Penn Hollar, in comments to an earlier draft of chapter 3, 9 October 2009. Used by permission.

Chapter 4—If You Do Not Wish to Become Pregnant, How Will You Prevent It?

1. Dan Ariely, "The Influence of Arousal," chapter 5 in *Predictably Irrational: The Hidden Forces That Shape Our Decisions*, rev. ed. (New York: HarperCollins, 2008), 89–108.

2. Jim Bob and Michelle Duggar Family Web site: duggarfamily.com/faq.html; accessed October 10, 2009.

3. http://www.vatican.va/holy_father/paul_vi/encyclicals/documents/hf_p-vi_enc_25071968_humanae-vitae_en.html; accessed July 20, 2010.

4. http://www.rxpgnews.com/health/Abstinence_Education_Programs_Have_No_Impact_on_Sexual_Beahviour_23770.shtml; accessed November 9, 2010.